$aved

HOW I QUIT WORRYING
ABOUT MONEY *and*
BECAME THE RICHEST GUY
in the WORLD

BEN HEWITT

Rodale books may be purchased for business or promotional use or for special sales.
For information, please write to:
Special Markets Department, Rodale, Inc., 733 Third Avenue, New York, NY 10017

Printed in the United States of America
Rodale Inc. makes every effort to use acid-free ♾, recycled paper ♻.

Book design by Amy King

Library of Congress Cataloging-in-Publication Data is on file with the publisher.

ISBN 978-1-60961-408-9 hardcover

Distributed to the trade by Macmillan

2 4 6 8 10 9 7 5 3 1 hardcover

We inspire and enable people to improve their lives and the world around them.
rodalebooks.com

"My riches is life."
—BOB MARLEY

CONTENTS

ACKNOWLEDGMENTS

I FEAR it would be impossible—or worse, unforgivably tedious—if I were to list everyone who has contributed to this book, either in person or through the sharing of their ideas and insight via their own works. Therefore, I will keep this relatively brief.

First, I am tremendously grateful to my friend Erik Gillard, both for opening his life to me and in the process demonstrating what true wealth looks like. It is no exaggeration to say that my friendship with Erik has transformed not only my relationship to money, but also my understanding of what simply *matters*. This is one of the greatest gifts I have ever received, and it is my deep hope to pass along his generosity to as many people as possible.

Second, I would like to thank the people who juggled the pragmatic aspects of bringing this book to life. These include my amazing agent Russell Galen, whose insight was essential to the process, and my editor Mike Zimmerman, who granted me the freedom to allow this book to unfold as my experiences dictated. I am also particularly indebted to a pair of insightful and sharp-eyed readers, Mary Elder Jacobsen and Woden Teachout. Thank you, all.

Finally, I am profoundly grateful to my family, including my wife Penny and my sons Finlay and Rye. Not only do they support and nurture me during the writing process, they are forever reminding me that the best things in life aren't things at all. As if that weren't enough, not a one of them ever complains that I don't make enough money.

PRELUDE

THE BOY is only 12 and already he is a cradle of self-awareness and resourcefulness rarely associated with such tender youth.

At 12, he is a vegetarian and has been for a year already, for he loves animals and cannot imagine their having suffered for his benefit. Or perhaps more accurately, he can imagine it, and because he can, he cannot be party to it.

At 12, he erects complicated structures in the backyard of his parents' home, utilizing materials scavenged from the cobwebbed corners of the old timber-framed barn that sits listing but still majestic in the center of the property. One of these structures is a tree house he built with his brothers, and when he speaks of it now, he describes like this: "We built it way up in the tree, like five stories, and it had all these platforms and windows and stuff." His hands dart and jab the air in the retelling, like birds pecking at scraps of food. Nearly 2 decades have unfolded since that tree house was built; perhaps the passing of time has made the tree house grander, as the passing of time is wont to do. But still: five stories!

At 12, he collects castaway bottles, in part because it bothers him to see them cast away, and in part because he likes to line them up in rows along the walls of his room. He thinks the glass is pretty, and he thinks that maybe someday he'll find a use for them.

At 12, he is walking home from school one afternoon and spies the top of a bar stool emerging from a dumpster. It is orange, like a traffic cone. Like a beacon. He grabs the rim of the dumpster and boosts himself up the smooth metal side. He grabs the stool, throws it over his shoulder, and carries it 1 mile home. It's a perfectly good stool, and he can't understand why it was thrown away, but he doesn't dwell on it. He is only 12, after all.

In the winter when he is 12, he skates every day on the reservoir only a few steps from his house. He thinks about how he learned to skate many years before, alternately wobbling and gliding across the ice, wearing a leather football helmet that once belonged to his grandfather. He remembers how his father would tie his skates for him, stooped over his feet in the open doorway of the barn, his father's fingers red with cold. Fumbling with the laces. This is one of his strongest memories, and in its recounting, his hands remain still.

He remembers how, years before, someone had released a school of goldfish into the reservoir, how they'd thrived, grown fat and sleek on whatever goldfish eat. He tells how, out on the ice, he pumped his arms and began to push outward on the honed steel blades of his skates. They cut shallow grooves on the reservoir's surface. Parting frozen water. Rhythmic scrape, blood rushing through him, he begins to move across the frozen surface, graceful, fast, unencumbered, unafraid. No helmet now. He doesn't fall anymore.

He looks down. The ice is clear, or at least clear enough that he can see the carp, grown now, each a foot long or more. They scatter beneath him and he tries to follow one and for a while it lets him, but then it veers downward and disappears in the murky water. For the briefest of moments he imagines himself a fish, living among a school of other fish. But it's silly, he knows. He is not equipped for such things and besides, they are down there and he is up here, separated by a barrier that is at once translucent and impenetrable.

He pumps his arms again, faster. He pushes his blades again, harder. He carries nothing; he needs nothing.

Has he ever felt so free?

INTRODUCTION

IN 2008, just as the financial crisis was revealing the full extent of its well-honed teeth, I came to a startling conclusion: I knew nothing about money. This gap in my knowledge was not exactly new, of course: I'd quite happily lived with it for the entirety of the nearly 4 decades I'd been alive. But in late 2008, having watched my meager retirement savings become half as meager, this ignorance suddenly felt like a burden I very much needed to lay down. *Where had my money gone?* I had a vague notion that it had been transferred to someone else, someone on the right side of a bet I was hardly aware I'd even made, but I wasn't sure. I mean, money couldn't just disappear. . . . Or could it?

The more I thought about it (and believe me, I thought about it plenty, for what else is insomnia good for?), the more I recognized how poorly I understood money. Not only did I not know where my fragile little nest egg had flown to, I did not really understand where it had come from, or what, even, it represented. I mean, I knew in the abstract that it could be used to purchase goods and services, things I needed, like toilet paper and gasoline, and things I didn't really need, but were awfully nice to have, like underwear and Internet access. I grasped that these things had value, which was denominated in and in large part defined by money.

But what if the money was just sitting there, not changing hands, not buying anything? What, then, was it worth? I suspected there must be something more to it than the paper upon which it was printed or (as is increasingly the case) the pixels comprising the digitized numbers flashing across my computer screen whenever I accessed one of my online accounts. But what that something more might be, I couldn't say.

Now, it was at about this time—with my IRA in tatters and my status as almost-middle-class freelance magazine writer threatened by the sudden closure of numerous titles that had previously graced me with a goodly amount of work—that I made the acquaintance of a man named Erik Gillard. Acquaintanceship soon evolved into friendship, and I became very familiar with the particulars of Erik Gillard's life, which, I was immensely intrigued to learn, did not include money. Or not very much of it, at least. And yet Erik immediately struck me as one of the most contented people I'd ever met. Was there a correlation, I wondered, between Erik's evident contentment and his aversion to money? I thought there could be, and with my paying work disappearing faster than a keg of Bud Light at a NASCAR race, I figured that at the very least, Erik could teach me a trick or two about living on the cheap. Given the increasingly sporadic nature of my paychecks, I was going to need all the cheap tricks I could get.

These coincident factors—the dawning recognition of my ignorance regarding money, my newfound friendship with a man who barely used it, and the alarming possibility that my primary means for acquiring the currency of 21st-century America was about to join Lehman Brothers in the dust bowl of financial history—seemed to me almost fateful. It also seemed to me like fascinating subject matter for a book. The result is what you are now reading.

As is so often the case, hindsight allows me to see just how naïve I was. Because when I actually starting writing about my friend and my evolving understanding of money, I quickly came to see I'd included only two pieces of a much larger puzzle. The story that was unfolding, I soon realized, was not so much about money, but about the *nature* of money. It was not so much about my friend's aversion to money, but his embrace of an entirely different form of wealth. In making these statements it may seem as if I am splitting hairs, but in the following pages, I promise to explain why and how I am not.

This book argues for an evolved definition and consciousness regarding our "economy," to the extent that at times it may be hardly recognizable as such. I am not talking about a "new economy," a phrase that is often associated with technology and the gauzy, seductive sense of prosperity we attribute to the digital era. Rather, I am talking about a perspective on economics that transcends almost everything we have come to associate with the word. The perspective I present may sometimes seem radical, but this is only because our current context for economics has become severely distorted by the paradigm of growth-dependent corporatism and the increasingly monetized nature of our lives and relationships. This is what I call the "unconscious economy," and, as I will argue, *this* is what's radical, for it can exist only when we ignore the most basic laws of nature and when we engage in the deepest self-deception.

Across the political and social spectrums there is little debate that there is a need to reform our economy and no shortage of ideas regarding how this might be accomplished. But the overwhelming majority of these ideas, no matter their origins or their details, are tragically flawed, because none of them address the underlying issues at play. In short, they assume the necessity and survival of the unconscious economy, even as it continues to erode the true, holistic wealth upon which all of humanity depends.

Perhaps the greatest challenge inherent in writing a book that attempts to redefine words and disputes the very premise of the ideas behind those words is developing the linguistic shorthand necessary to make it clear which definition is at play at any given time. Are we talking about wealth, or *wealth*? The economy, or the *economy*? I might have chosen to develop new words: "econocology" or "wealthonomy." But the truth is, rather than coining clever new words, we need to profoundly alter our relationship to the words we already have, and, even more important, to the associations contained within these relationships. I chose "conscious economy" because I feel it suggests, to the extent any two-word term can, what it is we need to do most: wake up to the fact that the economy we have been reared under is sadly lacking in its acknowledgement of basic truths. In short, it is unconscious.

The term "conscious economy" does not refer to our economy in the faulty and destructive way we've come to understand it, and it is also necessary to redefine "wealth" so that our cultural perceptions of the word are no longer dependent on systems and arrangements that undermine both the natural world and ourselves—which, as we will see, are really one and the same. In discussions of wealth, I have settled on "holistic wealth" to differentiate between the definition I will lay out and the status quo assumption of wealth as relating to monetary and physical assets (aka cash and "stuff").

Like so many of my fellow Americans, I am not comfortable with our nation's general trajectory. This is not to say there are no bright spots, such as the slow erosion of discrimination against racial and ethnic minorities. But on both macro and micro levels, looking out across the spectrum of politics, finance, environment, and even interpersonal relationships, I am troubled. There are, of course, numerous factors contributing to this malaise, but I have come to believe that most, if not all, of these factors are built on the foundation of our personal and collective relationships to money, wealth, and abundance.

In other words, no matter how honorable our intentions might be, no matter how diligently we work to repair what has been broken, or protect that which has not, we will be at best only marginally successful so long as we operate in the unconscious economy. Nowhere is this more obvious than in the realm of environmental protection, where despite the tireless efforts of innumerable activists and passionate citizens, the relentlessly dispiriting trends continue. In 2010, in the face of overwhelming evidence that anthropogenic climate change is one of the greatest crises we face, global carbon emissions jumped by a record 5.9 percent. During that same year, and not entirely unrelated to this jump in emissions, the earth lost an estimated 50,000 species—a pace that is 1,000 times the natural extinction rate.

Not surprisingly, most of this pollution, along with a majority of the species losses, can be attributed to habitat destruction wrought by logging, mining, agriculture, and other forms of industry that feed—and feed off of—the unconscious economy. Sure, for a while we might be able to halt (or at least stall) an oil pipeline or protect a particular habitat. But so long as we continue to inhabit an economy that must grow, so long as we continue to devote ourselves to the accumulation of monetary wealth, these measures will never be more than very small bandages on a very big wound.

This is a purposefully simplistic example, as befitting a short introduction to a book that greatly expands on the subjects of wealth (both holistic and not), economy (both conscious and unconscious), money (of every stripe), value, and worth. What is important at this point is not to grasp the minutia of the conscious economy, but rather to begin to understand, in broad terms, what I mean when I speak of it.

One last matter, before we dive in. This book is, in no small part, about a personal process. When I began writing this book, I thought I was writing merely about my friend Erik and his relationship to wealth. It should have come as no surprise to learn that what I was really writing about was *my* relationship to money and wealth and, by extension, all of our relationships to money and wealth. I did not know it at the outset, but what I was really writing about was the difference between value and worth, between true affluence and the hollow prosperity of the commodity marketplace that now provides and controls almost all of the material components of our very survival.

What I was really writing about, I came to realize, was how we might recast our expectations and shun the empty abundance of material affluence as we acknowledge and embrace true, holistic wealth. We inhabit a socioeconomic environment of historically high income and asset inequality, a nation cleaved by the 99 percent to 1 percent divide. But however unjust this may seem, and however fervently we might wish to balance the scales, I often wonder if those of us among the overwhelming majority of this split owe it to ourselves to ask a simple question: *Is this a form of wealth we even want?*

In short, this is what I hope to convey in the title of this book: We can choose to cut ourselves free from the artifice of monetary wealth. We can save ourselves from the damage such wealth causes, both to humanity and to the natural world. We can save ourselves from the burden of the need to pass the majority of our lives in pursuit of the money we need to procure the goods and services that, in an economy that has commodified practically every facet of our well-being, are essential to our very survival.

Of course, at times it can seem as if we have no other choice but to shoulder this burden. The unconscious economy has backed us into a corner, both individually and collectively, making us both its dependents and its curators. This influence can sometimes feel overwhelming and insurmountable, and it can seem as if the range of choices available to us is limited to only those we are offered by the commodity marketplace. But as we will see, this is merely a story we have been told. Whether or not we believe it is entirely up to us.

[CHAPTER ONE]

In which it is revealed that our happiness or lack thereof is often nothing more than a manifestation of our expectations.

LATE NOVEMBER in northern Vermont is a time of cold, snow, and a raw, ceaseless wind that howls across the landscape in unending curtains like a bad joke you've heard 1,000 times before. During this period, storms blow in from the northwest, one after another after another, gathering their anger as they sweep across the stolid gray waters of the Great Lakes. Or they spiral up the coast, sucking moisture off the oceanic surface—this they hoard and then deposit across the northern hills. Or (and this happens quite frequently) they erupt in localized bursts, provoked by moist air climbing the frozen mountains. The moisture rises, crystallizes and falls, rises, crystallizes and falls, a cycle not unlike schools of spawning salmon trying to overcome the cruel laws of nature.

It was in just such conditions that I arrived at the property of Erik Gillard, having parked my car at the edge of a snow-slick gravel road and set foot on a snow-slick path that unfurled beneath a canopy of towering pines. It was dusk, or nearly so, and the light possessed a spectral quality that was strangely welcoming, as if whatever ghosts might emerge would come only in kindness. The path was crossed at odd intervals by snarls of root; off to the right, a creek burbled along its wayward path, doing its slow work of eroding stone and soil. To my left, there was a small fenced-in plot where, the summer before, Erik had raised a few ducks. They were gone now. He'd eaten them.

I trudged up the path, drawing deep breaths of air and letting it settle into my chest, where it burned in a satisfying way. Snow fell through the pines, driven to a slant by the north wind. It was hard to tell if the storm was beginning or ending; it was hard to tell if it even was a storm. Perhaps it was merely a prelude for the winter to come.

At the end of the path I found Erik. He was bent over a pair of wobbly sawhorses, cutting through a wide board with a handsaw. His arm pistoned up and down and up again as he worked the saw, which made a sound that reminded me of water over gravel as its teeth removed a thin kerf of wood. The ground was littered with sawdust and cast-off pieces of board. A ladder leaned against a wall at a precariously compound angle: not just tilted out, as a ladder should be, but also tipped slightly sideways, as a ladder should never be.

Given the conditions, Erik wasn't wearing much. While I was clad in heavily insulated coveralls, pac boots, and a thick woolen jacket, he wore only a threadbare cotton sweatshirt against the cold. Its hood hung behind him, catching flakes of snow that quickly melted into the fabric. His feet were tucked into a pair of McEnroe–era tennis shoes that looked entirely inadequate for the snow-covered sheet of ice below him. His hands were ungloved. On his head, he wore a baseball cap, perched at an angle that precisely matched the ladder's ill-considered tilt. Was this an illusion? I closed my eyes for a moment, then opened them again. Nope. No change.

I stood and watched for a minute, a span of time marked by scant progress on Erik's part. To my admittedly inexperienced eyes, it looked as if the saw blade was caressing the wood, rather than cutting through it with the toothy abandon one might hope for. I could imagine myself, were I in Erik's tennis shoes, being driven to such frustration that I would send the saw in a great skyward arc, to its final resting place in the stream.

But I already knew him to be a man possessing the serene demeanor of someone with very little to lose. He had no other pressing obligations: If the saw were inclined to caress, rather than to cut, he'd let the damn thing caress. His arm kept pistoning—*up, down, up, down*—and the wood gradually gave way before it. A flurry of sawdust mixed and fell with the snow, carpeting the ground in white and brown. I could smell the freshly cut wood. It smelled like summer.

Erik Gillard was building a house, although he may have been the only one to ever refer to it as such. I, for one, could think of more appropriate descriptors—words like "shed," or "shack," or (generously) "cabin." It stood rather precariously atop small towers of cemented-together stone. Erik had pulled the rocks from the creek. It had taken 2 days to extract enough stone to form the pilings, and on the third day, he stayed in bed.

The house was two stories high, with a footprint of approximately 8 feet by 12 feet, although Erik was keen to point out that the bay window he'd installed had created almost an extra foot of floor space along much of the south wall. Certainly, the window generated a welcome bit of breathing room, but either way, I'd never seen so small a house. It was a caricature of a house, like something you'd inhabit in a dream where everything but you has shrunk and you can't figure out how to fit into your tiny pants.

There was, as of yet, no heat source. Nor was there a front door. Erik did own a woodstove; it was tucked into a moldering yurt that sat a dozen or so feet downhill from the house. He did not own a front door but thought he might build one, and he wondered if I had any idea of how that might be accomplished, and fairly quickly: He hoped to move in sometime next week.

The house did not feature running water, nor would it ever. The toilet was a bucket and the bucket was situated outside, behind the structure—there, "structure" is a nice, unambiguously polite word for it—under two old doors that had been tipped against each other, forming a triangular shelter. I tried to imagine myself hunched under those doors on a cold winter's morning, exposed to whatever elements the day saw fit to expose me to.

Frankly, the structure, which he hoped to complete for less than $5,000, was a substantial step up from his prior residence, a $400-per-month rental he'd shared with his friend David, a young man who'd made quite an impression on me when I'd visited Erik some months before. This was for two reasons. For starters, he'd had one of his front teeth capped in pure gold. In rural Vermont, this is not something you see very often. Indeed, it was my first gold-capped tooth sighting in all of my 40 years, and I must admit, I was utterly transfixed by the damn thing. It was like a campfire, or a car accident: No matter how hard I tried, I couldn't look away. Perhaps that was the intended effect.

Second, and almost as interesting, was David's affinity for working out with a kettlebell. Kettlebells, if you're not familiar with them, are nothing more than orbs of cast iron welded to a handle. They look, vaguely, like truck nutz—the die-cast testicles that fans of country music like to hang from the rear of their pickups. David had a preference for complicated circular motions, but first he would dip and bend, his breath deepening and rushing past the gold tooth, which glinted in the light of the room's single bare bulb. Then he'd rise and begin swinging the 35-pound ball from side to side, a frenetic, almost violent activity that caused me to duck and wince. I could not help but imagine the kettlebell slipping from his sweaty hands and gaining momentum as it smashed through the air between us, on a trajectory that bode poorly for me.

Yes, it's true, that place had a sink and a toilet, and a big old woodstove radiating delicious waves of heat. These were its strengths, but they were also its weaknesses, for the sink and lavatory were nearing the bottom of a long slide into decrepitude (Had these guys never *heard* of toilet bowl cleaner? Did they not *understand* what the flush handle was for?), and the floor around the woodstove was pitted with deep black burns caused by errant embers. Upon noticing these, I'd cast about for a fire extinguisher and, not finding one, had made studious note of the nearest exit.

And then there was the smell. It was a startling blend of kimchi, a fermented vegetable medley that was enthusiastically bubbling away on the kitchen table, and the gamey vapors of David's kettlebell exertions. Some of it came from the bathroom, where the sharp, mineral-rich scent of urine originated. There was something else in the air too, but when it comes to such odors, there is a point at which you're better off not knowing. I had reached that point.

All of which is to say that Erik's new home, despite its obvious shortcomings, represented a strange form of upward mobility for the man. It was small, cramped even. When he nailed on a piece of siding, the whole place shuddered a bit, as if it could actually feel the nail piercing its woody flesh. His toileting was subject to the whims of nature; even his drinking water would need to be packed in. Legally, the place wasn't even his, for it had been built on land owned by a friend. There was no electrical service to the site; my friend's nights would be forever lit by the smoky glimmer of candle and lantern.

As I watched Erik ascend the ladder, freshly cut board in one hand and a hammer in the other, it occurred to me that the whole scene should have been fraught with a sense of desperation and longing. Who, in 21st-century America, could accept such conditions in the absence of these emotions? Who could poke his head into the doorless doorway and not feel as if he were squeezing himself into a child's playhouse or perhaps a shelter for a small species of farm animal—goats or pigs, maybe? Who could stand out in the freezing gloom of a late-November afternoon, noodling through a wide board with a blunt handsaw, who else but someone in the throes of chronic pathos? Even more puzzling: *Why* would a person accept these things, not merely in resignation, mind you, but with what appeared to be genuine enthusiasm?

Because to hear Erik talk about it, you'd think he'd just finished picking out what color countertops he wanted and deciding whether the entertainment room should be finished in cherry or pine. And what of the landscaping? A cobbled driveway, perhaps, lined by shrubbery? A flower garden, or just some window boxes? It was here, taking majestic shape before him. It was real, for he could reach out and touch it and even, just barely, stretch to his full length along its end wall. Best of all, it was his. I mean, sort of.

"I'm so, so pumped to have my own place," he told me. He lowered his voice a few decibels, as if there might be something embarrassing in what would come next. "This is kind of a dream for me." Erik turned his back to me and drove a nail into the hand-cut board. The house shifted slightly on its footings but quickly settled. And Erik reached for another nail.

In 2009, the year I first met him, Erik Gillard earned about $6,000 from a part-time job at a children's wilderness camp. And managed to save a good bit of it. In 2010, the year he turned 26, he received a substantial raise, one that would put him on track to earn nearly $10,000 for the year. When he told me this, he sounded almost embarrassed, as if no one person should be entrusted with so much money. "Oh well," he said. "I guess with the house, it'll be good to have some extra cash around." I considered sharing the particulars of my income, but thought better of it.

This may be giving away too much, too early, but I think it's important for you to know that Erik is not a kook. Nor is he destitute, or desperate, or depressed. Indeed, he is the least of these things of perhaps anyone I know. He is healthy and strong, articulate and obviously intelligent. He does not smoke or consume alcohol, and he is careful about what he eats, in the sense that he does not eat very much processed food (in another sense, one that we will get to, he is not careful in the least). He does not even drink soda, or at least, I've never seen him drink a soda. He exercises regularly, though of course not at a health club. He is usually, but not always, clean. Frankly, sometimes he smells a bit ripe, the inevitable result of living without running water. He has a girlfriend, a sweet-faced and even sweeter-natured woman named Heidi. She is from Wisconsin and is the embodiment of northern Midwest charm. Often, she and Erik sing together. Her voice is lilting and ascendant; naturally, his is deeper, with a kind of innocent power. They've been together for 2 years now. It wouldn't surprise me if they got married. It wouldn't surprise me if they didn't.

Erik Gillard is a man of many skills. He is particularly good with children (this is good, given that his career, such as it is, depends on his being good with children), and he is tremendously proficient in the wild. He can build a fire with a bow drill, tan a deer hide using the animal's brains, or construct a weather-tight shelter of twigs and leaves. He is an amazing and versatile visual artist: paintings, drawings, carvings. He does them all, and he does them well. He's obviously no carpenter, but he built a house, or at least a cabin, anyway. He might have said, "I don't know how to build a cabin," which would have been fair enough, because he didn't. But that's not what he said.

The point I am trying to make is that Erik is not a loser. In one sense, he is the poorest person I know. It may already be obvious that in another sense, he is the wealthiest. It is not hard to quantify his poverty; it shows itself in the cold, objective numbers of his salary and bank account. It is more difficult to take measure of his wealth, which does not present itself in such ready terms.

That we carry assumptions about the poor, that we stereotype, generalize, and perhaps even discriminate, likely comes as no surprise. One of those generalizations is that people—and in particular, Americans—don't want to be poor, that poverty makes them feel bereft, lesser, hollowed out, victimized. One of the things that intrigues me about Erik Gillard is that for him, poverty seems to have the opposite effect. The less he spends, the less he needs to make. And the less he makes, the less money that flows through the river of his life, the more fulfilled he seems to feel.

Why is this? Is there something wrong with him? I'm pretty sure not, but I intend to find out for certain. How did he get this way? Does he ever have regrets?

Or what if I have it exactly backward: What if it is not his poverty that brings him happiness, but his wealth? Because already it is becoming clear to me that Erik considers himself extraordinarily wealthy. Do not think that he is delusional, or simply contrarian; instead, understand that he does not view money as an emblem of wealth, nor any material asset that would demand he subjugate himself to its accumulation. It's not that he doesn't like stuff; indeed, he has possessions that he likes very, very much. Loves, even. But they tend to be things that have been given to him by friends or family, or that he has created himself, and thus it seems reasonable to wonder if what he likes about these things is not the objects themselves, but the relationships they represent.

In other words, they are symbols of their underlying value.

Which is rather strange, if you think about it: because that's exactly what money is.

I often wonder if the tale of Erik Gillard's self-imposed frugality might serve as a fable. It is hard not to consider his life in the context of our nation's economic plight and its relationship to money and thrift.

There's no need to dwell on the obvious, but it is nonetheless worth noting: America is, for all intents and purposes, broke. Now, one might argue that our nation still enjoys an abundance of intellect and ingenuity, still draws from a deep pool of resourcefulness and grit. On these points, you'll hear no argument from me; these have always been our nation's strengths, and I believe they always will be.

But when it comes to money, the numbers don't lie. Our country has exhausted its savings and has resorted to spending its future income. Everyone seems to acknowledge that as business plans go, this one is not particularly sound. Yet we seem to have been struck dumb by the force of our desire for it to not be so, and rather than act, we continue shuffling toward an unspoken consensus about whether or not to fight for a way of life that we love dearly, but which we know has no future.

Why is it so hard to imagine a different way? Maybe it's because most of us have known nothing but expansion; the last of our Depression-era grandparents have passed on, leaving only stories that fade into the march of time, become diluted and fragmented by the long sweep of plenty. We know there have been times in our nation's history when money has been exceedingly scarce; between 1930 and 1933, during the onset of the Great Depression, the US money supply contracted by nearly one-third. The sudden loss of so much monetary wealth had devastating implications, of course. But it did something else: It focused attention on wealth outside the monetary realm. How many times have you heard or read a Depression-era account that includes this statement: "We didn't have any money, but we were rich"?

Still, that was 75 or more years ago, and much is forgotten over three-quarters of a century. Among other things, we forget that it hasn't always been this way. And with nearly 8 decades of relative stability and bounty having interceded between the Great Depression and early-21st-century America, we stop being able to imagine that it might not always be so.

Of course, the past 5 years have begun to alert us to this possibility, but the truth is the erosion began nearly a half-century ago. "I can't imagine there has ever been a more gratifying time or place to be alive than America in the 1950s," Bill Bryson writes in his memoir, *The Life and Times of the Thunderbolt Kid.* He goes on to support his assertion with a list of statistics that, given our current woes, is almost cruel in how devastatingly it illustrates our country's fall from grace over just the past few decades. Perhaps most tellingly: In the '50s, 99.93 percent of the vehicles on American roads were built in America, by Americans. Even the gas we pumped into our fleet of Buicks and Oldsmobiles was a product of the homeland, for in 1950, the United States imported just 8.4 percent of its oil. Nowadays, GM sells more cars in China than in the nation of its founding. Which is probably a good thing, considering that we now import nearly 70 percent of our oil.

This downward spiral is not confined to our highways. Of the major countries composing the Organization for the Economic Cooperation and Development (OECD)—including Canada, France, Germany, Japan, the Scandinavian countries, and the United Kingdom—the United States owns the dubious distinction of possessing the highest poverty rate, the lowest score on the United Nations' index of "material well-being," the highest homicide rate, and the largest prison population in both absolute terms and per capita. And that's just to name a few of the categories in which we fall flat on our flag. It's important to remember that each and every one of these dubious distinctions was in the making long before our current economic predicament. In other words, even as Americans have in aggregate become richer, we've become poorer, too.

It's not hard to imagine why someone like Erik Gillard might wonder if there's a better way, and if he can make a satisfying life in the margins of an economy and culture that seem destined for a reckoning. It's not hard to imagine why he might view the pursuit of the modern American Dream, with its big house, big car, and big debt, as something futile, vulnerable, and even damaging. If he can find happiness in the absence of these things, why shouldn't he? If he can feel pride and even joy at the raising of a $5,000, 96-square-foot house on a piece of borrowed land, why would he ask for more? Is Erik Gillard 22 times *less* happy than me, in my 2,200-square-foot home? The answer, of course, is no.

Through the lens of contemporary American culture, it's easy to view Erik Gillard as an outcast, or perhaps a relic. And in the context of the false prosperity of the past decades, that may be true. But this country was not built on monetized prosperity; it was built on toil, thrift, ingenuity, resourcefulness, and simple grit (it's worth noting that it was also built on violence and the displacement of native peoples, but the two are not mutually exclusive).

But think about it for a minute: Like America, Erik is pretty much broke. And like America, he possesses an enviable degree of intellect, ingenuity, resourcefulness, and grit. In this regard, and surely without realizing it, Erik is a true patriot, a man who personifies the best of traditional American values, even when doing so is inconvenient or uncomfortable. And he does so at the precise time when our nation needs to embrace those values more tightly than it has for many, many years.

It is probably worth noting that this is not how Erik views himself. Erik's view, if he's asked to articulate it (and if he's not, he won't; he's not a proselytizer), is at once simpler and more complex. The simple version is not that America has abandoned the virtues mentioned above, but that it has applied them in ways that are detrimental to its people, its environment, its spirit, and its psyche. It has taken these virtues and used them to build systems of great complexity and, it increasingly appears, vulnerability. In doing so, it has concentrated money in the hands of the few. The way Erik sees things, the most effective antidote to this predatory arrangement is to apply those selfsame virtues in pursuit of an opposite outcome.

This may be obvious, but Erik does not believe our country is headed in a promising direction. In this regard, at least (and rather depressingly), he is in the majority. He sees the ills propagated by the misapplication of our so American virtues. He sees the physical degeneration caused by junk food, stress, car culture, and the nearly three dozen hours of television we watch each week. He sees the high unemployment, and the outsourced jobs that leave his fellow countrymen and women with empty days and sleepless nights. He sees the almost utter disconnect between us and nature and the almost absolute disregard for the eternal rhythms that we might ignore, but which we cannot escape. He sees people trapped in their 4,000-square-foot homes, fooling themselves into believing they are free, when in fact they are imprisoned. By a mortgage, by the two jobs necessary to service that mortgage, perhaps even by the house itself.

He sees all this, and he is determined not to be a part of it. And then, along with a growing contingent of his fellow Americans, he thinks: It can't last. It won't last. And even: It *shouldn't* last.

There is an inevitable conclusion to all of this. What if Erik Gillard is the norm, and the rest of us are the outcasts, fooled by our majority presence into believing that we embody something deeply historical? If ever we desire validation that our decision to inhabit a big house and to work 60-hour weeks in order to pay for it is a sound decision, we need only turn on the television (if it wasn't already on), or look around us. And we hardly question the widespread assumption that wealth and security are defined by numbers in a bank account. We are told to save for retirement, to save for our children's college education, to work and hoard and invest for a future that will otherwise be one of impoverishment and fear.

Of course, the economic and social arrangements we know today have scant historical precedence, and it was not long ago that our investments were not primarily fiscal in nature. We invested in property, to be sure, but also in less tangible assets, like trust and community. We understood that we could not stand separate from others in our communities, nor from the natural world that provided the foundational essentials for day-to-day survival. Often, we coaxed those essentials from the land with our own hands, and we knew this to be its own sort of wealth: the knowledge and physical capacity to provide for ourselves and others. We lived modestly, perhaps even poorly by today's standards, but rarely felt bereft. Our consumptive expectations had not yet been set by the rush to capitalize on the productive capacity of the early 1900s.

All of which is to say, our current understanding of wealth-as-money is a foundling thing, and the historical precedence regarding both affluence and expectations tilts steeply in Erik's favor. We have lived through something of an aberration, whereby rapid extraction of natural resources and expansion of credit have perverted our collective definition of wealth. But in recent years, we have entered an era of declining natural resources, ever more costly energy, and credit deflation; as such, our adulterated definition of wealth will by necessity change. To which there is only one conclusion: Perhaps Erik Gillard does not merely represent an evolved sense of prosperity and contentment. Perhaps he represents something that is both profound and affecting to us all. Perhaps he represents our future.

If this seems rather far-fetched and generally unlikely, please understand that I am not suggesting that someday soon we will all inhabit 96-square-foot homes. I am not here to argue that Erik Gillard, with his bucket toilet and four-figure salary, is the literal embodiment of our future. Rather, what intrigues me is how Erik's version of affluence might inform a more connected and ultimately richer society. To do that, of course, it must inform us individually, and if I'm to be honest (and at the risk of sounding selfish), this is what intrigues me most: What might *I* learn from Erik? How might he help me better understand what is real wealth and what is illusory? And how might this understanding help me feel more secure about my family's future, and also the future of those around me? Finally, will this security enable me to inhabit the moments of my life more fully and with greater satisfaction?

In short, what I hope to understand by studying Erik Gillard is not a sense of what we stand to lose by downsizing our expectations and recasting our definition of wealth, but a sense of what is possible to *gain*. Naturally, the particulars of this are different for each of us, but what can be gleaned from Erik's story is, I believe, universal.

On that first afternoon visit to Erik Gillard's new home, toward the end of daylight's brief battle with dark, I pointed to his inadequate footwear, which by then was soaked through. "Nice shoes," I said, but my tone was sarcastic, for even in my insulated boots, my toes were curled against the cold. Surely Erik had noticed my warm boots; surely he'd silently compared them to the ragged, wet sneakers he wore and then found his own foot protection lacking.

Erik glanced down at his shoes, as if truly seeing them for the first time. Then he looked back up at me. "Yeah," he said, his face beaming. "I found them in the trash. Aren't they great?" If he'd noticed the sarcasm in my comment, he gave no indication. He lifted a foot out of the gathering snow, so that I might better admire his score.

This, I believe, is the most compelling thing about Erik. He makes every discovery, no matter how modest, how lacking, how downright cheap, feel like the most wonderful, promising goddamn thing in the world. When I'm with him, I find myself infected by the same view, and my sense of optimism seems suddenly boundless and unconquerable. I feel fully immersed in the moment, in a way that is too often lacking in my life. What is it that pulls me out of the moment over and over again? Often, it is anxiety over the future. Sometimes acute, but more frequently lingering and hardly acknowledged, the almost ubiquitous low-grade anxiety of preparing for the days, years, and decades that we all hope stretch out before us. We need money, we think. We need this and we need that. We must accumulate these things so that someday, we can exist free of the need to accumulate these things. So that someday, we can occupy our lives to the extent we know is possible, but cannot afford just yet.

I probably do not need to point out that this is a trap.

When I take leave of Erik, I am able to hold on to this optimism and sense of security for a time. But slowly, inevitably, it fades. Slowly, inevitably, I am pulled back into the eddy of my life. Mine is not a bad life; indeed, it is a very good life and I am happy. But I am not inherently blessed with the gift of Erik's modest expectations, and I often sense that I am lacking the resourcefulness and grit that enable him to thrive on so little. I feel that my expectations are too high, and my happiness too dependent upon them being met. I worry about the future, and

I think about accumulating money to protect myself from this worry. And I resolve to change this.

In the doorless doorway of Erik's house, we stood for a moment, regarding his feet as the dark gathered around us. The snow had stopped falling, and the air was still and softer than earlier. Before long, it would snow again. But for now, the storm was over. I looked up, past Erik, toward his house. Its lines had faded into the backdrop of the night, and it no longer looked small or comical. It just looked like a home.

[CHAPTER TWO]

In which I begin to consider my relationship to wealth and how monetary concerns have come to dominate 21st-century American life.

IN 2010, the year I started writing this book, I made $35,145, before taxes. This is just a bit more than half the median household income in my home state of Vermont, which for that year was $66,598. I am married; my wife's name is Penny, and we have two sons, Finlay and Rye. We all live in the same house. We compose, by any reasonable measure, a household.

In 21st-century America, $35,000 is not considered a particularly generous sum on which to support a family of four, although of course it is far above the poverty level ($22,350) and it is enormously more money than many of the world's households will see not just in a year, but a lifetime. In the context of our financial well-being, I must admit it was a pretty good year for me; although there have been a handful of years in which I've done somewhat better, there have been many more in which I've made quite a bit less. Still, I struggle to recall with any degree of accuracy which years were flush, and which were not, and I can only conclude that this failure suggests my good years were not really *that* good, and my bad years, not *that* bad. Either that, or my memory is going.

And what did I do to earn my 35 grand? Mostly, I wrote, as I am a self-employed writer and run a small farm on 40 acres in northern Vermont. While there is much to recommend about this particular career path, stability of income and abundance of monetary recompense do not generally make the list. I am no Bill Bryson or Jonathan Franzen. When folks hint about my capacity to earn a full-time living from the written word (as they inevitably do, with barely concealed suspicion that my "writing career" is a front for either a trust fund or something more nefarious), I liken my career to that of the touring bar band, playing gig after gig, collecting the meager proceeds as a squirrel collects nuts. Always on the proverbial road, always hustling, always shushing the keening voices in my head, telling me that each gig might be my last. The farm, I assure you, provides little in the way of financial remuneration, although its value to me usurps traditional metrics of money and profit (and it saves a heck of a lot of money that would otherwise be spent at the grocery store). I will have more to say about this later.

The point, really, is that my 2010 earnings represent an average or even slightly better than average year's wages for me and, as such, provide a convenient starting point from which to begin examining my relationship to monetary wealth. In pragmatic terms, it is enough to ensure that my family remains well provisioned in the day-in, day-out essentials of 21st–century American life. It even allows for the occasional frivolity. But it is also a modest enough sum to ensure that finances remain an almost-constant consideration, and this is despite the fact that for most of our adult lives, Penny and I have worked diligently to reduce our dependence on money.

Sociologically speaking, it is roughly the correct amount of income for our community, which is to say, it is an amount that allows us to feel a certain kinship with our working-class friends and neighbors in rural Vermont, most (but sadly, not all) of whom, like us, are free from immediate concerns of hunger and shelter, but not from longer-term monetary worries. There are few here who have entered the hallowed realm in which one's money does the earning for them. In these parts, folks largely depend on their physicality to pay the bills, and it is often evident in the way they move: a limp, a hitch, a stoop, a barely concealed wince upon rising from a chair. They've given more than time and perspiration in pursuit of money.

In short, we do not stand apart from our neighbors in either poverty or wealth, and for this I am grateful. In a small community like ours, income disparity and wealth accumulation are particularly evident, as are the social dichotomies they create. I'm not suggesting I live amidst a firestorm of ongoing class warfare, only that subtle classism exists in my hometown, as it does in most communities. To be among the majority class is of no small benefit, even if that entails subsisting on a modest income.

It will be helpful to us both, I think, if I am entirely candid at this early stage: I do not even like money. Except, that is not quite true, because it's not *money* I mind so much, as the suffocating sense that like most human beings in the modern world, I am obliged to spend so much of my life in pursuit of it. And that this pursuit is going to in large part define the particulars of my adult years, and not merely the 100,000 or so hours I'll devote to earning, but also so much of what revolves around those hours: where I live, who I know, even *what* I know. All of these are defined at least in part by career choices that are very often made for strictly financial reasons.

I do not mean to suggest that one must dislike one's work (although, depressingly, the majority of working Americans do), or feel enslaved by one's career. In fact, I know that just the opposite is true, because I truly love my job. Most days, I even manage approach it with a reservoir of gratitude, although of course some days that reservoir is deeper than others. Nonetheless, I am grateful for my work, and not just for its earning potential. I realize how lucky I am to be able to say that.

Yet I cannot deny a certain degree of resentment that money—or a lack thereof—commands so much of my attention and generates the overwhelming majority of the strife I experience. I cannot help feeling somewhat bitter that, no matter how hard we try, no matter what deprivations we endure (and there have been plenty, I assure you), Penny and I remain beholden to the monetary realm. I am bothered by the fact that for the majority of my adult life, I have fretted over money. And then, ridiculously, I fret over my fretting: Why have I allowed myself to worry so much? I have never gone hungry, or spent a night unsheltered from the elements. I have never even been at risk of these things. Most of my worry, I have come to realize, has emerged from a place of uncertainty and fear. Not over the present, mind you, or even the medium-term future, but over the belief that I should be accumulating monetary wealth in preparation for an unknown future. Why? Because it's what I've been told I must do; it's what we all have been told we must do. And so we collect the nuts, trading our time—which is to say, our life—for them, and squirreling them away and then worrying about whether or not they're squirreled in the right place, at high enough return, to enable us to live the life we someday hope to live.

Finally, I cannot but resent the fact that our economic and monetary systems have evolved to a place that divides our nation's people into the haves and have-nots, and that the latter comprise the overwhelming majority of us. *We are the 99 percent*, as the saying goes, and if it's true—if there really are 99 of "us" to every 1 of "them"—it is a dispiriting indictment of the arrangements that have given risen to such disparity. Because with such resounding strength in numbers, wouldn't you think change would come quickly, if not easily? I contend that the fact that it does not says more about our country's health than the fact that such a division has arisen in the first place.

It is instructive to consider income inequality in an historical context. In 1928, immediately preceding the Great Depression, the richest 1 percent of Americans pulled down 24 percent of the country's total income. The Depression and its resultant policies had a leveling effect, and by 1976, the richest 1 percent earned "only" 9 percent of total income. But the past 30 years have been particularly good for the one-percenters, who again command a disturbingly familiar portion of our nation's income pie: 24 percent.

Still, I wish for you to not think this is an "us versus them" book. I have no interest in fomenting conflict or fueling a cultural divide that does not lack for tinder. So yes, I admit to the aforementioned simmering resentments, but I chose to focus that resentment on the study of how I—and by extension, others—might refocus our attention. Instead of clamoring for more of our share of wealth within the context of a system that seems entirely uninterested in redistribution, might it behoove us to imagine how we might become less dependent on such things? What if we could liberate ourselves from that suffocating sense of being chained to a financial system that we *know* is preying on us, and yet that we feel powerless to escape?

I am not preaching the prosperity gospel, or if I am, it's not a prosperity that can be measured solely in numbers. In fact, much of my interest lies in exploring what an evolved version of prosperity might look like and what might enable us to realize such a thing. Over the past few years, as the financial divisions in our nation have become ever starker, and the burdens of propping up a deeply and intractably flawed system shifted ever more onto the backs of those least able to shoulder the load, I have come to believe that reimagining wealth is not only beneficial, but inevitable. It *will* happen, whether we choose it or not. It occurs to me that to proactively usher in this transition is a far better thing than to have it imposed upon us, either by mandate or natural order.

To be clear, I am not suggesting that money should not and will not be a constituent part of this prosperity, and so I am also interested in how our monetary system has evolved and how it might evolve further. I am intrigued by my relationship to money, and how it informs my relationships to others and to the natural world. I sense that these relationships do not always benefit from my use of money, and in fact might be outright damaged by it, but as of yet, I'm not sure exactly how this could be.

And there's this, which I have hinted at but perhaps not overtly enough: I cannot help but wonder if the assumed version of wealth, replete with the means to call forth on a whim whatever goods or services one might desire, actually bespeaks a certain poverty. Rich in anonymous, homogenous things, the gadgets that compel us to camp out on city streets, just so we might be among the first to have a phone we can talk to. Siri, will you be my friend? The expansive houses we endeavor to fill with IKEA's particleboard furnishings, designed to appeal to common denominators of mass desirability: conveniently flat-packed, assembled with ease (but not too easily, lest we are made to feel inept—even production furniture, it seems, understands the value of playing hard to get), and styled for universal approval. Cheap, easy, and impersonal. But the space is never truly filled; the need is never truly met. Because the space and need are not to be found inside the shell of our homes. Indeed, they are to be found inside of us.

If I'm right about all this, it could be said that we are both wealthy and poor, as our contrived needs are met over and over without lasting gratification. For proof of the latter, I offer as evidence the constant desire to upgrade and renovate, to obtain and accumulate. Little of this trade is in essentials; most of it is in goods that despite ardent promises to the contrary only complicate our lives and widen the divisions between us and the natural world upon which we ultimately depend. Which is no less a part of us than our very hands or heart. We feel iPhone-poor because we are, in fact, I-poor: Our sense of self and feeling of connectedness have become fragmented and eroded, and so we turn to the easy pickings and short-term relief provided by industry and peddled by masters of emotion-based marketing. But our poverty is one that a talking cellular telephone, for all its digitized genius and touchscreen sensuality, can never heal. In fact, it will only make things worse.

What I do not yet know is how our monetary system contributes to both our wealth and our poverty, which we can already begin to see as two sides of the same coin. I do not yet understand how our money system works and how it is that money itself can be both abundant and scarce. To be honest, I'm not always sure why we need money at all, for it seems at best little more than a human contrivance mediating between us and our needs, and merely a symbol of the real value it is intended to represent. Even the short-lived $100,000 bill—the largest denomination of currency ever issued by the US Treasury—is by itself worthless. It is only via a collective agreement and faith in our government that any of our currency and coinage, down to the lowly penny, holds any value at all. Maybe this is important; maybe it is not. Certainly, it is an aspect of our money that intrigues me.

In recent years, as I have begun to grasp how profoundly our narrow view of wealth damages us, our communities, and the environment (as if these can really be placed into separate categories), I have found myself struggling to articulate how we might contemporize and redefine this definition for the betterment of all. This book is part of my attempt to write that definition. But I know that I can't do it myself, and my hope is that if I keep my eyes, ears, and mind open, Erik Gillard will help me find the right words.

[CHAPTER THREE]

IN WHICH I GO MUSHROOM HUNTING WITH ERIK AND BREAKFAST, THEREBY PROVING BENJAMIN FRANKLIN WRONG.

IN LATE May of 2011, at 9 o'clock on a Thursday morning, a man named Breakfast piloted an elderly Honda station wagon up a steep gravel road somewhere in rural central Vermont. It was a warm day, knocking on hot, and the sun shone brightly in a cerulean sky. This was a welcome change from the weather of the previous weeks, which had been unyieldingly damp and raw, as if winter couldn't quite accept that its time was over. If there were a finer morning to be chauffeured through the springing Vermont countryside by a man nicknamed after the morning meal, I'd yet to experience it.

Only 90 minutes before, I'd received a call from Erik. "I'm

going morel hunting with my friend Breakfast," said Erik, speaking into the phone he'd mounted at the base of a telephone pole down the road from his new home. I drifted for a moment, conjuring an image of him crouched by the pole, telephone receiver pressed to his ear. Naturally, it was a corded phone, so he would be unable to wander. I suspected he was sitting on the ground, leaning his back against the pole; I'd noticed that Erik always seemed to seek contact with the ground. "Want to come?"

"I don't know," I said, because truly, I didn't know. Like most people in 21st-century America, I generally plan my days ahead of time, and on this Thursday I had somehow neglected to include a note to "go mushrooming with Erik and Breakfast" on my list of tasks. It was a forgivable lapse, I'd argue, given that it was a weekday and that, like most people I knew, I had work to attend to. But I was beginning to learn that if I wanted to spend time with Erik, I was going to have to be flexible because he wasn't like most people I knew.

"I don't kn—" I started to say again, and then: "Did you say '*with my friend Breakfast*?'"

Erik acknowledged that indeed he had, and it suddenly seemed to me as if perhaps there was nothing more deserving of my attention than the opportunity being put before me. Suddenly, I could not imagine any excuse good enough to warrant passing up the opportunity to hunt Vermont's esteemed morel with Erik and Breakfast. That's because, of course, there wasn't.

As he drove, Breakfast suckled from a gourd of yerba maté, a twiggy tea that smelled like something kept in the dark too long. He lounged in his seat, a moderately heavyset man of 30, his skin marked by perhaps the least menacing menagerie of tattoos ever worn by one person. They were loosely organized around a food-related theme: an eggplant, an homage to coffee, and, my favorite, the words "SNAK TIME" spelled out in capital letters across the back side of his fingers, gangsta style. The "c" had been eliminated so that Breakfast's message to the world would fit on the eight digits that were visible when his hands were clenched into fists, and I had a chuckle imagining the poor, confused sucker whose last sight before Breakfast's punches rained down upon him was the phrase "SNAK TIME." Part of what made this funny was that Breakfast was one of the least-menacing people I'd ever met; far as I could tell, the only danger he posed was to a mature morel mushroom.

And this is how I found myself seated next to Breakfast, as he nursed from his gourd and steered the Honda with his "SNAK" hand. We were headed for one of the boys' most reliable and prolific morel hunting grounds, which spanned the flank of a small mountain only minutes from Erik's home. Not for the first time, I was struck by how Erik managed to extract so much pleasure from such a limited range. He wasn't a stick-in-the-mud; he made regular trips to his childhood home in southern New Hampshire, and on occasion, he even traveled outside New England. Still, I'd never met someone so appreciative of and knowledgeable about the small piece of world outside his doorstep. He knew where and when to find the most prolific patches of fiddlehead ferns and wild nettles. His hands would sting when he picked them, but it was worth that small pain for the pleasure they would bring, steamed and slathered in butter. He knew where certain animals lived and where large, south-facing rocks protruded from the ground to absorb the heat of the sun. It felt good to sit and lean against them, to allow the warmth to radiate into his body. Come August, he would know precisely where to find the best swimming holes, those refreshing icy pools that lie far off the beaten path, where he'd shuck his clothing and immerse himself in the water, feeling the cold radiate throughout his body like a low–voltage electrical current. And in the winter, he'd head out on his skis, gliding through towering stands of maple and ash, the snow pristine but for the tracks left by moose and porcupine and, in the aftermath of his passing, himself.

Of course, he knew where the morel mushrooms bloomed and when—middle spring in Vermont. Like most fungi, it grows almost comically fast; it's not uncommon for the species to put on 3 or 4 inches overnight. It's a homely bugger, having the misfortune to be at once wrinkled, brown, and oblong, but its questionable aesthetics don't translate to its flavor, which is at once meaty and earthy; think beef tenderloin crusted in dirt. My earliest introduction to the morel came courtesy of my grandmother, who gathered them in the woods surrounding her farm in southeastern Iowa. I have a vague recollection of the smell of them frying in her kitchen, although that might have simply been the smell of her kitchen, which in the 1970s Midwest was a room largely devoted to the heating of Crisco to the melting point and beyond. I remember following my grandmother through the Iowa woods in search of them as she regaled me with the story of an encounter with a copperhead and I tried not to scream every time I saw a curved stick.

In any event, it would be more than a generation before the morel and I would meet again. This time, it would be courtesy of Erik, in the certifiably copperhead-free (though timber rattlers make occasional appearances) hills of Vermont, and I was honored by the immense show of generosity on his part for having invited me. Generally speaking, mushroom hunters are a secretive, if not paranoid, lot, and this generalization doesn't even account for the fact that on this day, we were after the Holy Grail—the one wild mushroom that reigns over all others in the hierarchy of fungal desirability. The morel is the reclusive celebrity of the mushrooming subculture; sightings are often validated by photographic evidence, and hunts are exhaustively detailed on Internet forums dedicated to the subject.

But as I had found to be the case with almost everything that Erik does or owns or otherwise perceives as falling under his purview, his prevailing ethos was one of generosity in the extreme. Withholding something as valuable as explicit directions (What could be more explicit than leading me there?) to a first-rate morel repository was as unthinkable to him as denying a cup of water to someone dying of thirst. It wasn't that he didn't hold the mushrooms in high esteem; actually, it was the opposite, for in Erik's view, something as tangible (you can see, hold, taste, and smell a mushroom) and pragmatic (mushrooms are food, after all) as a morel is a true and honest representation of value, more so than perhaps any amount of currency. Moreover, to Erik the time spent hunting the morel was not something to be calculated and then subtracted from whatever appraisal might be assigned to the final haul; rather, the search itself contributed to the mushrooms' intrinsic worth, even if that worth could not readily be articulated in numeric values.

For his part, Erik put it a bit more simply: "It's so fun to walk around and look for things that may or may not be there," he said at one point late in our ramble up, across, and ultimately over the mountain.

And it *was* fun, although I must admit to no small degree of frustration at my inability to spot the things that may or may not have been there. Only minutes after Breakfast parked at the road's shoulder and we set foot into the forest beyond, my two companions were scurrying from one patch of the coveted mushrooms to another, while I scanned the ground furiously and mostly futilely, trying to establish visual parameters for distinguishing fungal growth from the backdrop of the previous autumn's fallen leaves, which composed a nearly uninterrupted carpet of brownish organic matter. Sensing my gathering angst, Erik pointed toward a stand of mushrooms, or what I presumed to be a stand of mushrooms. Frankly, I couldn't tell; they might have been piles of dog shit for all I knew.

"See, there's some," he said.

I squinted. "Where?"

"There."

I squinted some more, until everything began to get dark the way things get dark when you close your eyes, thus defeating the purpose.

"*Where?*" I said again, and it must have sounded to Erik as if I might cry, for he all but took my hand and led me to the bounty.

Lo and behold, there they were: my first morels, although it's really not fair of me to take any credit for their capture. After all, an expert 'shroomer had led me by my nose, and not merely to the general site, but also to these specific mushrooms, a quartet of wrinkled fungi I quickly and mercilessly liberated from their resting spot. I did this without compunction, as I'd done a bit of research into the subject of mushrooming and knew that the aboveground morel is merely the "fruit" of an expansive network of a rootlike structure called mycelium. While it is beneficial to leave at least some intact mushrooms to spread their spores for future generations (and because it would simply be greedy to take 'em all), it is difficult to overpick any particular spot, since the mycelium is the actual organism from which the mushroom grows, and there's no practical way (or logical reason) to take that. Harvesting apples from a tree is an apt analogy, I suppose.

Per Erik's suggestion, I'd worn a baseball cap, not so much for protection from the elements but because, when removed and carried upside down, it formed a convenient mushroom satchel. I removed it now, and dropped my stash into the makeshift bowl. I stared at my prize a moment; they really *were* ugly, but they captivated me nonetheless, if only because I knew my hat contained something that transcended the caloric value of the mushrooms therein; I knew that all across the region—perhaps on this very day, at this very hour or even minute—mushroom hunters, cameras cocked and loaded, were combing the woods for the elusive morels. *And I had some.*

I am ashamed to say that a rush of self-congratulatory contentment washed over me as I gazed into my brimming hat. I could actually *feel* it passing through my body; it was cozy, like slipping into a bath on a dark January night. Still, I am even more ashamed to say that I'm fairly certain my reaction was based not merely on the satisfaction of finding the morels, but on the fact that I had something others wanted. This does not speak well of me, I realize, but at least I had the good sense to stop myself from sharing this view with Erik and Breakfast, who would surely have found it crass. But what can I say? I'm only human, and no more so than in the small-mindedness of this humble victory over an untold number (but surely, *surely* it was a large number) of morel seekers.

Having held the quarry in my bare hands seemed to somehow tune my eyes and psyche to the task at hand, and for the first time I experienced "mushroom eyes." I'd been introduced to the term by another mushroomer; he'd uttered the words with quiet, almost whispering reverence, as if the words and the powers they described were so fickle, they deserved the benefit of superstition and could not be spoken of loudly enough that the mushroom gods might overhear. At the time, I'd merely nodded dumbly and a bit dismissively, because the majority of devoted mushroomers share a common loopiness, the mild madness of the obsessed, and are fairly easily dismissed. But now I understood precisely what he'd meant. It was if my eyes were an instrument; where before they'd been playing slightly out-of-tune, now they rang in harmony with the world around them.

An exaggeration? Not at all, because suddenly the morels stood in sharp relief to a backdrop that had previously rendered them all but indistinguishable. This is not to say I saw them everywhere; even in a hot spot such as this, morels are relatively scarce. But whereas I'd previously felt uncertain and tentative, I now felt quietly confident, almost predatory. Whereas before I'd tiptoed through the woods, hoping I'd be blessed enough to catch a glimpse of something that might or might not be there, now I stalked and prowled, absolutely certain the mushrooms were there, equally certain I'd find them, and very much assured of my right to claim them. My hat was nearly full, but I wanted more, more, MORE.

I shook my head, and hard. Goodness. What was happening to me? Somewhere deep inside me, in a place where emotion usurps intellect, the morels had triggered a compulsion to accumulate and, perhaps even more alarming, hoard. Because I wasn't much interested in sharing my little (hopefully soon to be large) stash with anyone but my family. I wanted to return home with not just a hatful but a bagful, and a garbage bag, at that. I wanted my family to admire my treasure and remark over my prowess. Hell, I thought I might even post some pictures on one of those Internet forums.

In one sense, this all seemed innocent enough: Morels are desirable. It was my first hunt, and I could be forgiven for displaying the enthusiasm of a neophyte. But in another sense, it seemed little more than a mirror of the very behavior I had come to see as problematic and even amoral. So I had to wonder: Is it merely human nature that compels us to amass so much more than we truly need, even in the face of mounting evidence that doing so actually undermines our well-being? Maybe, I thought, we just can't help it.

This was a dispiriting line of inquiry, from which I was gratefully distracted by the discovery of yet another patch of mushrooms. I'd figured out a key secret to finding morels: They are extremely fond of standing dead elm trees, and almost as happy growing in the soil of abandoned apple orchards. In mushrooming parlance, the elm and apple are "indicator trees," which is to say they are indicative of a relatively high probability that morels can be found in the surrounding soil. This is good news, because it's a hell of a lot easier to spot a standing dead elm or an apple tree than to find the mushrooms themselves.

With this bit of information tucked into my small holding of mushrooming knowledge, and the focus of my mushroom eyes shifting confidently between the ground and the tree canopy, it was as if I'd been invited to a private morel party. Within 20 minutes, my hat was overflowing, and I moved through the forest with one hand clenched around my impromptu mushroom bag, and the other pressed against my chest, cradling half a dozen specimens in the shallow hollow of my ribcage. I wished like hell I'd brought a camera to document my incredible success, and I could already imagine myself at some future party, holding court over a rapt audience: *And then, just when I thought that surely there couldn't be even more . . . here, let me show you some pictures.*

Erik had long ago filled his hat and removed his shirt, despite the clouds of blackflies that accompanied us through the forest. I'd always thought of him as skinny, but now I saw that he carried an ample supply of muscle. It was not the sort of puffy, cultivated musculature developed in the cold fluorescence of a gym; rather it was as if his limbs and torso had been purposely built to do what human bodies were originally intended to do: Hunt. Forage. Survive. His body mirrored the stripped-down nature of his relationship to abundance; the superfluous had been jettisoned, leaving him with precisely what he needed and little more. I'd long before embraced the notion that Erik's frugal nature was good for his emotional health; now, I saw that perhaps it was good for his physical health, too.

This wasn't a particularly revelatory theory, but it did make me feel a bit better about the simple fact that I was, well, tuckered. By this point, we'd been tromping through the woods for 2 hours or more, and little of the ground we'd traversed had been flat. It wasn't as if I was suffering unduly, but my feet hurt a bit and my legs felt mushy, as if they'd been subjected to a tenderizing implement. The truth is, I'm fairly tough; I once completed a bicycle race that required that I remain awake for 36 hours straight, about 7 of which I spent actually racing. Not only that, but of the few hundred racers in attendance, I'd completed the fastest lap of the course. Like I said, tough. Yet here I was, pulling up the rear, and by no small margin. The fact that Breakfast had found the rust-pocked head of a 12-pound maul emerging from the carpet of leaves (Where the hell had that come from? There was no telling and no logical explanation, and yet, there it was) and had been lugging it around for nearly an hour did not make me feel any better.

I consoled myself with the belief that our hunt was nearly over. We'd found numerous pounds of morels, an enviable haul by anyone's measure, and this was exciting to Breakfast and Erik. Breakfast had the maul, and this seemed to please him no end. Why, all he needed was to fashion a new handle for it, and he'd be smashing the bejeezus out of whatever he pleased. Erik had donated an unknowable but substantial quantity of blood to the area's blackfly population; even those little buggers had gotten something out of the deal. Surely it was time to bring our adventure to a close; surely Breakfast and Erik had obligations to attend to. My own feeling at this point was basically that hunting morels was fun and all, and, to be sure, I was still looking forward to the tales I would tell, but also that mushrooming was a somewhat frivolous pursuit, and not something to which an entire day should be devoted.

Alas, my companions did not share this unspoken belief, and it was a full 2 hours more before we finally emerged from the woods, having circled almost the entirety of the hillock (Or was it a mountain? I couldn't decide, but whatever it was, it was steep), before cutting straight up against the fall line and clambering over its grassy dome. Along the way, we'd passed through a long since abandoned apple orchard, where blossoms and diminutive white moths filled the air, and it was only after I caught one of each in my hand that I could tell them apart. We'd also stumbled into a small clearing where an uninhabited cabin was beginning the slide into a state of decrepitude that would eventually return it to the earth. Erik explained that he had actually lived in the cabin for a time, and by now I knew him well enough that hearing this did not surprise me in the least. I asked how long it took to reach the road, walking the most direct route.

"Not long," he said. "Maybe 20 minutes."

I pondered this response for the next while, as we slowly corkscrewed our way toward the summit. *Not long, maybe 20 minutes.* In and of itself, it was an unremarkable answer, but remember: He was talking about 20 minutes of walking, each way, from his home to where he parked whatever dilapidated vehicle provided his motorized transport. The path he walked twice daily wound through the woods, through the same abandoned apple orchard we'd just passed, where blossoms and moths danced in the air. There was little more than a slight impression on the forest floor and a break in the forest understory to mark the route.

I imagined Erik walking through the orchard every day, on his way to and from the outside world. I imagined what it would be like to start my day passing through an orchard with blossoms falling on me, so weightlessly gentle that if I closed my eyes, I wouldn't know where they'd hit me. I thought about the sensation of my feet sinking ever so slightly with each step into the spongy layer of forest detritus that covered the ground. Before, I'd been tired and ready to go home, but now I felt energized. I tightened my grip on my cache of morels and scurried forward.

Even as I caught back up to my companions, I knew I was coming dangerously close to romanticizing Erik's daily trek. And not just the trek, but also everything having to do with the freedom afforded him by his exceptional thrift. Had there been days he cursed that damnable walk, days he hurried down the mountain path as fast as his feet would carry him, days when the falling blossoms and fluttering moths brought no more pleasure than the quotidian, even mundane events of his life? Surely there must have been, and I wanted to ask him, but already he and Breakfast were pulling away from me again, carried up the hill by legs and lungs better tuned to the task than mine.

I decided that I *was* romanticizing things. Still, the inescapable and somewhat unsettling conclusion remained: Erik's relationship to time was different from mine, and I say "unsettling" because I was fairly certain his relationship was less dysfunctional. I'd first noticed this more than 6 months before, during that November day I stopped by his house to find him contentedly cutting boards with a dull handsaw. During our mushroom hunt, I'd twice noted it, first when our search continued past the span of time that seemed (to me, at least) reasonable and again in response to my query about the hike from the cabin. There was something in the unhurried nature of Erik's day-to-day existence that made it feel as if he *owned* his time to an extent that most of us have forsaken.

In his book *Discretionary Time: A New Measure of Freedom*, Robert Goodin points out that time is both inherently egalitarian (everyone has access to the exact same 24 hours per day[1]) and inherently scarce (no one has access to *more* than 24 hours per day). Goodin talks about "temporal autonomy," which is the ability to make choices regarding how one's time is passed. Given the egalitarian nature of time, not to mention its scarcity,[2] the capacity to choose how we spend our time could be viewed as the ultimate expression of wealth, and it struck me that Erik's unhurried, almost languid temperament suggested a particular confidence that could only evolve from an abundance of temporal autonomy. Or, put more simply, from the certainty that he could damn well do what he pleased, when he pleased.

For a moment I probed my memory, but I could not recall a single instance when I'd heard Erik worry or even wonder about the time. And I thought how interesting it was that watches have become such a symbol of status in our culture that people are willing

---

[1] Of course, in the longer term, time is not so egalitarian, since not everyone lives for the same number of 24-hour days.

[2] "Scarce" in the sense that most people wish for more time, not less, so that demand for time typically outstrips supply.

to spend thousands or even tens of thousands of dollars on a little clock to ride on their wrist. Perhaps it was merely the jeweled aspect, the diamond-studded bezels and gold-striped bands, but I couldn't help wondering if it was also something in the auspicious display of the timekeeping mechanism itself, as if reminding the world that the bearer's time is so very valuable as to demand such royal carriage. And then an irony struck me: If one's time is so damn valuable, why in the name of Rolex would anyone allow a *clock* to rule it? Viewed in this light, being beholden to a clock could be seen not as you owning your time, but as your time owning *you*.

It occurred to me that unlike most of us, Erik does not compartmentalize his time; he does not seem to differentiate between the hours spent in pursuit of a paycheck and the hours spent in pursuit of either mushrooms, a finished cabin, or a pair of dumpster'd sneakers. He seemed to understand more clearly than anyone I'd met that there is only one thing human beings truly own, one thing that cannot be claimed by others: time. Furthermore, he seemed to respect the rather uncomfortable truth that none of us can rightly claim to know how much we own. As such, he seemed determined not to convert his unknown quantity of time—in truth, his life, for how we spend our hours and days is, of course, how we spend our lives—into a commodity, to be sold to the highest bidder.

At first, I struggled to square this with the languor he applied to so many of his tasks. For who would spend hours cutting boards with a rusty handsaw but someone who felt as if time were very much on their side? If Erik were really so cognizant of the true value attached to the ticking clock of his life, would it not behoove him to at least get a freakin' Skil saw? But the more I observed him in action, the more convinced I became that I had it exactly backward. Indeed, it occurred to me that Erik had an absolute respect for time, to the point that he was able to exist inside any particular moment with tangible contentment. He understood that the value wasn't to be extracted by rushing to get to the next project, but rather by truly inhabiting each and every moment he was fortunate enough to experience.

I recalled a brief exchange we'd had some months before, regarding the accepted truism that time is money, which, it will not surprise you to hear, Erik does not accept. It was Benjamin Franklin who was supposed to have first introduced the axiom, in his *Advice to a Young Tradesman.* "Remember that time is money," he wrote. "He that can earn ten shillings a day by his labour and goes abroad or sits idle one-half of that day, though he spends but sixpence during his diversion or idleness, ought not reckon that the only expense; he has really spent, or rather thrown away, five shillings besides."

Here was a depressing assertion. Had I really just thrown away nearly half a day's wages? I wondered, as I trudged up the hill. (And where the hell were Breakfast and Erik, anyway? I seemed to have lost sight of them.) The problem in answering this question was twofold. First, how to quantify the value of the time I'd spent in search of mushrooms? By the value of mushrooms themselves? Perhaps. But even if I were to arrive at a figure based on the fair market value of whatever portion of the day's haul I would be allotted—by now, all of our mushrooms, including my own meager holdings, had been comingled in a large paper shopping bag retrieved from Breakfast's car—I would still be left to wonder, if only because of the atypical nature of my actual, paying work. As a writer, I am not paid by the hour or by a fixed annual salary. Sometimes, I am paid by the word, with no regard given to the time it takes to link those words together into coherence.[3]

---

[3] My father, who is also a writer, likes to joke that this is why my work is full of very short words, such as "a" and "it." And also why I endeavor to include stutterers in my stories.

Sometimes, I am paid by the project, again with no fixed or even approximate expectation of the hours spent bringing the project to completion. Complicating matters is the fact that my annual income varies from year to year, sometimes drastically.

In short, I could not conceive of a logical nor convenient way to measure the monetary value of my "labours." Clearly, by spending much of the day mushrooming, I'd gotten myself sucked into a significant diversion, at least when contrasted against the writing work that comprises so many of my waking hours and pays to keep my family warm, dry, and fed. The slow, wretched burning in my leg muscles and the raw, scraped sensation in my lungs when I breathed deeply—which was every time I breathed—were proof enough that I had not, in fact, been idle. But still I could not shake the feeling that I had indeed thrown away, if not sixpence and five shillings, then *something*.

Troubling as this was, it was made even more so by yet another of Franklin's proverbs: "It takes money to make money." (Actually, that's not exactly what he said. He said: "Remember that money is of the prolific, generating nature." Which is pretty much the same thing.) If money is of the prolific, generating nature, and I'd just thrown away an unquantifiable amount of it, what had I really lost? In other words, how much money would the money I hadn't made *have* made if I'd made it? You can see the quandary I was in. My mind reeled with the implications of it all. And for nothing more than a few damnable mushrooms. How quickly and profoundly I'd sunk from the self-congratulatory heights of my first moreling success.

Now, even as I mulled over all this on that late May afternoon, I knew I wasn't engaging in particularly original thinking. There are no doubt plenty of people who understand that time and money are not so readily conflated, and furthermore grasp that the notion they can and should be is particularly convenient for the corporate entities that would very much prefer we exchange our time for the money necessary to purchase their offerings. In a sense, "time is money" could be capitalism's rallying cry; given the broad cultural agreement that it's true, perhaps it is.

So on this front, at least, I knew I wasn't onto anything revelatory. But there was something else niggling at the edges of my consciousness, something that I hadn't before considered, and it related to Franklin's assertion that money begets money. If this is true—and indeed I think it is, one only need consider how modern financial investment instruments work—then can the same also be said of time? In other words, is time of the prolific, generating nature? I don't mean literally, because of course one can't actually *produce* more time. But clearly one can allocate time, and to the extent that time allocated in the manner of your choosing feels like time *gained*, whereas time spent in subservience to others feels like time *lost*, then in a sense, one can create time simply by allocation. Even our contemporary lexicon suggests that we view time in this manner: When we are unexpectedly freed of an unsavory commitment, we speak of the time as something found, as if it did not previously exist.[4]

At that moment, trailing my companions through the forest, I was struck by a sensation I know well for having lived it repeatedly: the feeling that I am failing to simply appreciate my time and that this lack of appreciation is what allows it to slip from my grasp, over and over again. Most of us do this, of course. We somehow fail to recognize that life is just a collection of moments, stacked up one atop the other until they reach their inevitable conclusion. It suddenly seemed very clear to me that if I could learn to inhabit the constituent moments of my life more thoroughly, they would feel more substantial, more satisfying. And the more I did this, the

---

[4] Thinking even a bit more outside the box, we might consider that the very idea of time is a human contrivance, as is its measurement. In other words, does time even exist outside the boundary of ourselves? Or at the very least, does it exist in the manner in which we've come to view and measure it?

more I would do it, if only because it felt good. Like eating good chocolate, I suppose, only less likely to pad my love handles.

I knew I was treading on slippery ground, for how would I prove my foundling theory that it takes time to make time? Carry a stopwatch everywhere I go? And how to respond to the inevitable (and quite justifiable) argument that some people manage to spend their time in ways that are both financially lucrative and satisfying on a deeper level? In other words, how to know when to turn the stopwatch on and off? Because I'd seen already that Erik's chosen path demanded its own particular allocation of time: If he wasn't going to buy his food, he was going to have to forage for it, or grow it. If he wasn't going to buy shoes at a shoe store, he was going to have to procure them some other way, and this way was likely to demand a certain portion of his time. Of his life.

And yet I'd observed again and again how relaxed Erik seemed, how he never appeared hurried as the minutes of his life ticked by. More than anyone else I'd met, he seemed in command of his time and he rarely, if ever, gave the impression that there was something he'd rather be doing. Perhaps this was merely an attitudinal shift, an acceptance of (or, less charitably, an acquiescence to) the facts on the ground, so to speak. But isn't attitude shaped by the particulars of life? It struck me that Erik's relationship to time was a by-product of simple contentment, and that his contentment was, at least in part, a by-product of his decision to live as he wished.

Finally, I couldn't help but wonder if the accumulation of money and other dollar-denominated assets might cast a pall of anxiety over our leisure time. For who could feel good about leisure when every minute feels like a wasted opportunity? And if one is inclined to side with Mr. Franklin in the belief that time is money and that furthermore money begets money, how could one feel anything *but* anxiety when one's time is not recompensed in a monetary fashion?

Except, what I observed in Erik was almost precisely the opposite: He seemed to possess a deep reservoir of trust that his immediate needs would always be met. Because of this, he was uninterested in accumulated wealth (after all, if he could always trust that his immediate needs would be met, he could therefore trust that his *future* immediate needs would be met). Under these circumstances, what was to be gained from denominating his time in dollars? Freed from this perspective, he was also free to inhabit any particular moment fully and without guilt that it was somehow being frittered away.

This pondering was all starting to become a bit too intellectual and interior for me and besides, it all hinged on a wagon train of assumptions, observations, and unconfirmed (worse yet, unconfirm*able*) theories. But I could forgive myself. For one, I was fatigued and massively hungry; even a raw morel would have tasted good, if only I could've caught up to Breakfast, who was ferrying the load and seemed to be always either 20 paces ahead or to the side of me. Still, my musing had a not-inconsequential fringe benefit: Without my noticing it, we seemed to have nearly gained the summit of the little mountain; when I looked up the hillside, I could see open sky through the trees, like a beacon. Indeed, I was right, and in a few moments, we emerged from the forest and onto a grassy plateau from which we could see for many miles, in many directions. A narrow footpath wound across the hillock and we followed it to a favorable vantage point. Erik and Breakfast plopped into the grass, while I performed a few vaguely yogic stretches, hoping to ease the kinks from my back and lessen the sensation that someone had spent the past few hours peening my quadriceps with a large hammer.

It was quiet. Even Breakfast was quiet, and by now I'd spent enough time with him to understand that this was a rarity. Erik plucked a dead blackfly from his belly button and flicked it into the breeze. I leaned, rather fluidly I thought, into a complicated twisting position, and endeavored to hold it, which I did for 10 exceptionally long seconds, at which point I unwound myself, dropped to the ground, and sat for a minute or two, trying desperately not to ask the question I knew I was nonetheless about to ask.

"Hey," I asked, keeping my voice low and casual as I stood up. "Does either of you guys know what time it is?"

But, of course, neither of them did.

[CHAPTER FOUR]

In which I explain how I met Erik and became intrigued by his relationship to money and wealth.

I MET Erik Gillard in 2008. I liked him immediately, as did my wife, Penny, and we soon inquired as to whether he might mentor our boys in wilderness skills. Both of our sons had displayed a keen interest in the primitive; they wanted to create fire with bow drills fashioned from tree branches, hunt rabbits with homemade arrows, and sleep in stick-and-leaf shelters, having feasted on the very beast they'd brought down only hours before. Every time we passed a mangled lump of road-killed raccoon or woodchuck, they clamored for us to stop and retrieve it, so that they might fashion something from its hide. (This in no small part explains why our car has utterly no resale value; it simply smells too bad.) These struck us as noble pursuits that would engage all of their developing facilities, and because Penny and I lacked these skills ourselves, we needed some help.

Erik accepted our proposal and thus came to be a weekly fixture at our home. He would arrive in the morning, do his thing with leaves and sticks and the occasional unfortunate furred creature, and hang around for lunch. The boys loved him, and it was not hard to see why, for he is one of those people who seems always able to muster the specific energy children demand and to express delighted interest in the particulars of their small worlds, without a hint of condescension or belittlement. In short, he is respectful of children in a way that feels genuine. And increasingly rare.

Now, I don't recall exactly how the monetary component of our relationship was established, but I do remember that fairly early on, Erik made it known that he did not wish to be compensated with money. This was interesting to me, although not exactly shocking or revelatory; after all, we had conducted informal barter with friends and neighbors before.

But the more I learned about Erik, the more intrigued I became. It wasn't so much the mechanics of his life, which were slowly revealed over our lunchtime conversations. Rather, it was the sense of contentment and satisfaction he emanated in the context of what I had come to understand was a life largely devoid of accumulated wealth. To be sure, there are seekers aplenty who pledge themselves to scarcity and deprivation, but this was not Erik. He had not aligned himself with any particular religion or movement; he had not forsworn any particular luxury or desire.

In fact, as we chatted around the old farmhouse table in our kitchen, it seemed the opposite: It became clear that Erik was pretty darn certain he was one of the richest sons-a-bitches ever to walk the face of the earth. Of course, he would never say such a thing; already, I'd come to understand that his capacity for hubris was exactly zero. So there was nothing he *said* that gave me cause to believe he felt wealthy; it was more a matter of what he embodied and the way he seemed so thoroughly in command of his time. He rarely, if ever, was hurried; often he would linger, either over the remnants of lunch, or when engaging with the boys long after our agreed-upon time had elapsed. They would draw, or write in nature journals, or carve something out of a piece of wood liberated from the forest floor. Eventually, almost languidly, he'd lace up his dumpster'd tennis shoes, amble out to his mufflerless, $500 Volkswagen, and rumble down the road.

I understand that this must all seem a little vague. Here I am, claiming this fellow is one of the wealthiest people I've known, without any tangible evidence to validate my claim. This is the challenge inherent in defining a form of wealth that is not based on money or other physical assets: There is no convenient metric to fall back on. If I were to say, "Erik Gillard is the richest man I know; he has 118 bazillion dollars in the bank and owns a half-dozen beachside villas," you'd know exactly what I mean. But when I say, "Erik Gillard is the richest man I know; he is content and secure in the absence of money and seems to inhabit each moment of his life with great appreciation and awareness," it's a bit more difficult to sink your teeth into.

The ways in which our language has evolved and shifted to focus our attention on physical asset-based wealth has not escaped Erik's attention. "Economics is not just about the money economy," he told me one January morning, as we huddled around his woodstove, upon which a quartet of eggs sizzled in a small frying pan. The yolks were big and round and orange, small tangerines floating on white inner tubes. And they smelled maddeningly good. My stomach literally *mewled.*

Maybe I was distracted by sensory overload, but Erik's comment puzzled me. Was he espousing a personal theory or stating an inarguable truth? After all, like most Americans, I had come to think of economics as being *precisely* about the money economy. Hell, "money" and "economy" even sound similar. He continued: "Actually, the root of the word doesn't say a thing about money; it's about the management and study of the home." He flipped the eggs with a practiced flick of the wrist. Melted butter splattered onto the stovetop, and the air filled with a sweet smoke.

By this time, I'd come to understand that Erik harbored a deep repository of interesting and little-known information, and I'd learned that most of the time his information was factually accurate, or near enough so as to grant him the benefit of doubt. Still, this matter was so aligned with the thesis of this book that I felt compelled to do some fact-checking. Turns out, he was pretty damn close. The first part of the word *economy* descends from the ancient Greek word *oikos*, which taken literally referenced the household, although more popularly came to differentiate between what was private and what was public. The second part comes from the word *nomos*, used to describe pretty much any kind of law, be it of the personal, governmental, or natural spheres. Per Erik's contention, not a single mention of money.

It's not exactly uncommon for the meaning of a word to shift over time, but the fact that we have come to view economics and the economy as relating strictly to money strikes Erik as a particularly sad and damaging perversion. "People are always meeting their needs and managing their homes with 'economics' outside the money system. But no one sees that, or talks about it. In the popular sense, the economy has become all about Wall Street."

Semantics? Perhaps. After all, it's only language we're talking about; as Erik acknowledges, plenty of people are managing and regulating their private lives—or at least large swaths of their private lives—outside the dominant financial system. Just because they don't have a convenient term for the practice, doesn't mean they can't do it. To a certain extent, we all do because as it turns out, there really *are* some things money can't buy. But what we lack—what's been lost along the arc of the shifting definition of *economy*—is a convenient and universally understood way of talking about wealth and economics in nonmonetary terms. And to the extent that ideas are spread through language, this profoundly hampers our capacity to define nonmonetized wealth.

I first made Erik's acquaintance during a particularly tumultuous time for our country. The year 2008 was, to put it mildly, a period of tremendous fear and, for some, even downright terror. Job losses totaled 2.6 million, the worst since 1945, and the Dow Jones Industrial Average lost nearly 34 percent of its value, its third-worst year in history. Of course, the housing industry was swirling down the toilet bowl of history: In December of 2008, the Case-Shiller Index recorded its largest price drop ever.

I was not immune to the financial carnage; that same year a prominent magazine, for which I had been contracted over the previous half-dozen years to complete writing and editing services, was forced to cut nearly two-thirds of its staff. My freelance contract was not renewed, and in short order, I lost a position that I'd come to rely on for almost half my income. I managed to scrape together enough supplemental work to keep our household solvent, but like so many Americans, I was exposed to the sudden and unsettling understanding that I had very much to lose and worse yet, that *I might actually lose it*.

This fear, at least as it relates to that specific place in time and my family's long-term well-being, has since proven overblown (though not for a lot of people who *did* lose everything). Still, it is not hard for me to summon that sense of vulnerability, to retrieve it from the repository of faded emotion in which it has been stored. And it is difficult not to dwell on the possibility that such a crisis might well visit us again. Because what, really, has changed in the aftermath of the 2008 financial crisis? Not much at all.

I couldn't help noticing how unaffected Erik was by the storm surge of economic malaise, and I knew it wasn't simply a product of his easy-going nature. He seemed as if he really *didn't* have much to lose, at least not in the realm of material goods and financial investments. He had long since structured his life and set his expectations to thrive in conditions that by comparison reveal precisely how unfree most of us are. It is worth pointing out, I think, that these have not been the preparatory efforts of a man consumed by the decline of modern American society, but instead have evolved from a deep ethical imperative to live in just such a manner. Rather suddenly, it seemed to me like an imperative worth adopting.

For the record, Erik Gillard does not view himself as "frugal," "thrifty," "cheap," or "austere." He especially does not like the word "austerity," for he associates it with imposed cutbacks, the brunt of which are borne primarily by those least able to bear them. If there is something he wants very much, and he has the money to buy it, he will. It is worth noting, however, that he doesn't tend to want much, or at least not much that can be procured with money. During the 18 months I spent researching this book, he made the most expensive single material purchase of his life (in aggregate, of course, his cabin cost more). It was a used high-end touring bicycle, and it cost $675. It was not an easy purchase for him to make. "At first, I felt guilty," he told me. "And then I realized that the price equaled six workdays; six days in the woods with kids. Would I trade six days in the woods for this beautiful bike? I realized I would, and it affirmed to me that I am living a right lifestyle." While Erik waxed poetic, I did some quick math: $675 divided by 6 meant that Erik was making roughly $112 per day. Not awful, but not exactly a king's ransom, particularly given the part-time and seasonal nature of his job.

Still, there was something in Erik's retelling of the bicycle purchase that made me happy in a way I did not entirely understand, but I thought might have something to do with the fact that it seemed tinged by a sweet naïveté. To fret so earnestly over a purchase felt to me somehow old-fashioned, like a story told by my grandmother as she mixed a batch of cookies. Or, more accurately, hunted morels and bestowed me with a crippling phobia of copperhead snakes.

Or maybe it was that rather than simply fretting over spending the money—*should he, shouldn't he*—Erik had framed the decision to make the purchase in the context of his livelihood. Furthermore, his decision to buy the bike had affirmed his affection for his job and the manner in which he spent the minutes and hours of his paying work.

How many people, I wondered, think of purchases in this manner? How many people take the time to consider if any particular purchase is worth not just the money, but the portion of their life represented by the money? Erik had converted the abstract (money) to the concrete (him, in the woods, teaching children about nature), and the result had both comforted and buoyed him. I couldn't help but envy this. "Escaping the idea that work has to be toil is part of my privilege," he told me. "I feel as if I am privileged to live this way." This is as close as I've heard him come to flaunting the benefits of his chosen lifestyle.

It is important to note that when Erik speaks of privilege, he is speaking of entrenched societal privilege bestowed upon him by a structural hierarchy that by default does not deliver these advantages to all. (Otherwise, it could hardly be a hierarchy, could it?) Or as he explained it to me: "I am the same gender and skin color as those in the positions of highest power and domination, I have access to unearned cash if I were to really need it or as inheritance if my family were to pass on, I have afforded trust in relationships with folks who have access to resources with relative ease and often in a short time frame, and this also goes for interactions with cops, employers, clerks, teachers, and so on. I assume that some of this trust existed before me personally cultivating it, and was based simply on ways I look and am perceived in the context of terms engrained in society as the norm. I have access to land and grew up knowing the natural world, which has not been totally destroyed in the areas where I've lived. My first language is the dominant spoken tongue. If I were to need a job, I could probably get one pretty easily and one that paid well. My demographic and gender is portrayed as the winner and the hero in the media, and I'm likely privileged in ways I'm unaware of."

In short, Erik is not blind to the difficult truth that his chosen lifestyle, as bereft as it may seem to America's middle-class majority, is at least in part dependent on him having been born the "right" color, to the "right" ethnic group, in the "right" community. It may even be dependent on him being the "right" gender, with the "correct" sexual orientation. Put simply, he has *choices* that are not available to all, and the enviable freedom and connections he has forged for himself are the direct outgrowth of these choices.

I was somewhat embarrassed to realize how inadequately I'd acknowledged my own privilege and furthermore, how profoundly I'd failed to recognize the range of choices that were available to me. I'd like to think that I'm not to blame for my lack of awareness; after all, there is little support for such recognition and decisions in our culture, in no small part because our economy is dependent on very few people choosing similar paths. Indeed, it is not hard to see that our contemporary economy is largely dependent on consumers feeling *unprivileged*, and striving to match the standards set by those whom they perceive as being better off (one can only imagine what would happen to the stock value of, say, Home Depot if Americans suddenly flocked to 96-square-foot houses). My own dawning recognition that so much of what I had assumed to be necessary and true in regards to my relationship with money and material goods was, in fact, merely part of a cultural mythology that ignores a deeper truth: I was free to write my own fable. I was free to decide what affluence meant to me. My economy could be about much more than money.

Freedom's just another word for nothing left to lose, sang Janis Joplin, and although she managed to make it sound as if it arose from the ache of regret, I believe the greater regret lives in those of us who have lived as if the opposite were true. I do not mean to suggest that Erik Gillard has slipped the surly bonds of the moneyed economy, the ties of which bind even him, albeit much more loosely than most. But it requires little more than a cursory examination of America's troubled relationship with monetized wealth to feel the first, haunting pangs of envy for a life that is, by and large, not defined by the accumulation and dissemination of cash, credit, and other physical assets.

Of course, Erik has made sacrifices along the way, and his life is frequently made *more* complicated by his avoidance of accumulated wealth. Five-hundred-dollar cars leave him stranded, thumb out and shivering at the highway's edge; tasks that many of us would hire out to an expert require him either to seek out a friend in possession of these skills, or to learn them himself. Jobs that are merely tedious or downright onerous and that beg to be subcontracted become his domain. It perhaps goes without saying that Erik does not own many of the objects that have come to be contemporary society's assumed accoutrements or even necessities. He has no cell phone, no computer, no iPod or iPad. Since the retirement of his previously mentioned $500 Volkswagen, he has not owned a motorized vehicle, although he is granted access to Heidi's truck and, more recently, to his brother Ryan's old Toyota wagon. I've never seen all his possessions in one place, but I suspect that I would be somewhat shocked by how little he truly owns.

Now, it is altogether true that Erik's capacity to eschew material possessions is aided and abetted by others. He relies on family, friends, and community for the use of material goods (car, truck, computer, tools, and so on) that he has chosen not to procure for himself. In other words, a certain degree of his thrift and by extension his freedom is enabled by people who have chosen to be somewhat less thrifty. For a time this bothered me, as it seemed to me not merely ironic, but downright hypocritical. After all, if everyone chose to live on $6,000 annually, then who in the hell would we expect to be purchasing the things we could not afford, but occasionally needed to borrow? Or, as seemed to be the case with Heidi's truck, somewhat more often than occasionally.

I have come to view it differently, mostly because I have spent enough time with Erik to see how others benefit from his dependence on them. They benefit in pragmatic ways, such as when he returns a favor by helping plant a garden, or cares for an animal while its owner travels. But perhaps more important, they benefit from the gift of giving, of being depended upon. Of being, quite simply, *needed*. In the era of the commodity economy, with the capacity to call forth our needs and desires at a moment's notice, there are too few opportunities to be truly needed by others, to experience the satisfaction and simple warmth of being crucial to someone else's life. And it is important to note that Erik is conscientious and careful with other people's possessions. Once, when he'd borrowed his brother's car to visit our place, the muffler fell off. Erik was on the phone immediately, arranging for its repair.

I do not mean to suggest that by not owning things, Erik is not attached to material possessions. Indeed, it often appears to me that he is *more* attached to his belongings than has become typical in our culture, in no small part because their monetary value is often usurped by either their utilitarian significance, or the relationships they represent to him. I am repeatedly struck by the unalloyed delight he finds in the small treasures of his life, as I described at the end of chapter one. Except to him, they're not small. To Erik, a pair of shoes pulled from the fetid hollows of a city dumpster is as deserving of his gratitude as a pair of unblemished Nikes that have known not heel, toe, or sock. To Erik, a 96-square-foot home isn't so much 96 square feet, as it is a *home*. He fills his space with art and found pieces of nature: a gnarled stick, worn smooth by the elements; a heart stone, propped on a shelf; tiles his friend Janice made and gave him, depicting an owl and something that might be a rising sun or might just be a random arrangement of shapes that imbue their resemblance from the perspective of the individual. In short, he surrounds himself with things that are useful to him or that bespeak a connection to nature and to his community. Perhaps, even, his connection to *himself*: the pride he takes in his personal toil and resourcefulness.

We speak of materialism as if it were something bad and even sinful, but sometimes I wonder if we have it all wrong. Maybe what we need isn't less materialism, but *more*, to the point that we actually respect and even revere our material goods, rather than see them as disposable and constantly begging to be upgraded. Of course, it doesn't help that disposability is purposefully engineered into the overwhelming majority of the products offered to us. To seek out true quality requires the determination to look beyond the convenient venues of big box retailers and online mass merchants; needless to say, it also demands a willingness to pay for the upgraded materials and craftsmanship such quality demands.

From this vantage point, Erik Gillard might be the most materialistic person I know. The majority of the things he owns, despite their often being well used or even run down, seem to actually *mean* something to him. He uses them, to be sure: I recall a day in midwinter when I bumped into him at the little food cooperative where he does the bulk of his grocery shopping. He was bundled in his usual ragtag assortment of frayed woolens, aboard his new-to-him bicycle, the one that had cost more than the sum total of the three cars he's owned over the course of his adult life. The bicycle was coated in a scrim of ice and slush, and I was alarmed to see this: Mustn't this be damaging? Would it not suffer premature wear at the hands of the elements? How could he be so callous?

But as he rode away, piloting his bike with one hand, while clutching a small bag of groceries in the other, his legs circling in a rhythmic, almost hypnotic fashion as the raw wind began to push against his face and oxygenated blood coursed through his muscles, I recognized a deeper truth that allayed my concerns.

Erik had bought the bike to *use*, not to *have*.

In my most candid moments, I sometimes wonder if I would have found Erik's views on wealth and economics so compelling if our paths had crossed 2 years before, during the heady heights of the real estate boom, at a time when it seemed as if the Americanized version of prosperity, with its endless flow of cheap credit and ever–appreciating home values, knew no bounds. To be sure, even then I was afflicted by my debt phobia and fervently pursuing a lifestyle that would free me from its clutches.

Yet even I was swept into the current of the moment's false optimism; work was plentiful and seemed to find me with little effort on my part. Like any good capitalist, I exploited this situation to my full advantage, rarely saying no and often overcommitting. I commonly worked weekends and there were no vacations. It was during this period that we extinguished our mortgage, and the irony—if that's what it is—that the overblown state of our nation's real estate and credit markets played a significant role in the retirement of our loans is not lost on me. These were some of my most financially fruitful years, and I gleefully harvested these fruits, before utilizing them to buy our way out of debt.

Of course, on some level I was clearly predisposed to be drawn toward Erik's embrace of a more holistic wealth. Yet I cannot deny that almost immediately upon making his acquaintance, I found something comforting in the way he had structured his life, and I felt compelled to better understand how he made it all work. Very early in our friendship, against an economic backdrop that murmured "Greater Depression," I saw that Erik might serve as something of a mentor to me and that furthermore, this mentorship could be an ideal antidote to my suffocating sense that the financial world was imploding. And with it, my only means of supporting my family.

This is not to say I did not genuinely like the guy, because Erik is one of those people who are very hard not to like. He is approachable and unruffled, quick to smile and generous with laughter. He is not prone to broad swings of emotion, and his default countenance is one of reserved contentment. As he is with children—engaged and respectful—he is with adults, and despite living a principled life, he is one of the least judgmental people I've known. It is striking that, with the exception of those in the political and corporate sphere, I have never heard him speak ill of another person.

Look, the man is not perfect; I know that. Like all of us, Erik is beset with contradictions and inconsistencies. There are junctures in his life where his values are overwhelmed by his desire to participate in society. He drives cars that spew 20 pounds of carbon dioxide into the air for every gallon of gas burned in his service. He does not fly—not solely for environmental reasons, but because he finds the whole process, the pat downs and body scans, intrusive and demeaning—but he has no qualms about hopping a diesel-powered train and traveling to the Midwest to visit Heidi's family. He sometimes wears clothing hewn of synthetic fabrics that grace his back only via the very industrial supply chain he reviles.[5] He acknowledges these compromises and accepts them because he does not want to live in isolation or without some semblance of the common comforts of the 21st century. He is not a monk.

Nor am I, and it seems important to note that this story is not about a life of ascetic sensibilities. There will be no cave dwelling or communicating via smoke signals in the following pages; no one will be wearing a loincloth and subsisting on morning dew slurped from the hollows of leaves. Indeed, this story is precisely the opposite. It's an examination of a life that is profoundly abundant in ways that have become increasingly rare in contemporary America: freedom, community, choice, good health, and simple happiness.

It is also about the ways in which modern commerce, dependent on a monetary medium that by design establishes a profound disconnect between us and the natural world, creates the circumstances that ensure both wealth *and* poverty. Sadly, the wealth is too often in that which does not matter, and the poverty is frequently in that which does. And the irony of tragic ironies is that we are actually trading our real wealth for illusory riches.

My wager is that our culture is beginning to recognize that we have been on the losing end of this Faustian bargain. Somewhere in the back (maybe even nudging its way toward the front) of our collective consciousness is the recognition that all is not right with our relationship to money and wealth. We are beginning to understand that this dysfunction radiates outward, to our relationships to other people and to nature, and even inward, to ourselves. Somewhere is the sense that things are changing and that while this change may at times feel profoundly difficult, it is nonetheless as necessary as breathing. Having allowed so many facets of our

---

[5] I have even been told that, on occasion, he does not lower the toilet seat after use.

well-being to become monetized and commodified, we are presented the opportunity to reclaim these building blocks of true wealth.

The first step, of course, is to simply recognize them. This might well be Erik Gillard's greatest gift: to show us what these building blocks look like, and not merely in theory, but in the context of a real life. My premise is that the choices Erik has made—to live humbly, to eschew so many of the trappings of modern American life along with the debt that, for most of us, necessarily accompanies them—do not bespeak a diminished quality of life. Indeed, they bespeak a vastly *improved* quality of life, defined at least in part (but not solely, not at all) by the freedom he enjoys. Freedom to work as little or as much as he desires at a job he loves because it fills his soul with wonder and joy, even if it fails to fill his pockets beyond the bare minimum necessary to sustain his modest needs. Freedom to indulge his whims and muses, at least to the extent those whims and muses do not require financial resources he does not have. Freedom to disbelieve the adage "time is money," which strikes Erik as one of the dumbest things he's ever heard. Freedom to consider what constitutes true wealth and, better yet, freedom to pursue this truth.

For the full 40 years of my life thus far, a figure I dearly hope represents no less than the approximate halfway point of the time allotted to my physical being, I have remained mostly blind to the ways in which our contemporary definition of wealth disregards and even erodes the true riches of both humanity and the natural world. My blindness is not an anomaly; it is merely a reflection of a greater cultural ignorance that has been generations in the making. Exchanging this blindness for sight, on both individual and collective levels, is not an event, but a process. The first step is simply acknowledging that we are free to do so.

[CHAPTER FIVE]

In which I reveal all.

I WAS BORN on November 23, 1971, in a hospital in Saint Albans, Vermont, a small town situated in the midst of the state's northwest corridor, a flat and fertile swath of land that pushes against the flanks of the Green Mountains to the east and empties into Lake Champlain to the west. This is dairy farming country, although less so now than it was then. When I was born, Vermont was home to more than 5,000 dairy farms; today, there are fewer than 1,000, and they continue to dwindle at a rate of a dozen or so per year. Still, the ever-consolidating nature of the dairy industry means that those 1,000 or so farms are home to a tremendous number of bovines, and Vermont boasts more cows per capita than any other state in the union.

My arrival fell on the day before Thanksgiving, which has no particular bearing on anything but the fact that once every 7 years or so (leap years mess things up a bit), my birthday falls on Turkey Day. I've always felt badly for those whose birthdays fall on holidays, but if one had to choose a holiday to be born on, Thanksgiving is arguably one of the best because Thanksgiving does not inherently honor the birth of anyone else. Moreover, unlike Christmas, there is no traditional exchange of gifts, a practice that understandably imbues all December 25 birthdays with a needling doubt and subsequent confusion: Is this a Christmas gift, or a birthday gift? Did I end up with the same amount of gifts, more gifts, or fewer gifts than I would have if I'd been born on a different day? You can see how this could be damaging.

I was my parents' first child; at the time, we lived in a drafty old farmhouse set on 170 acres, at the edge of a gravel road not far outside the small town of Enosburg. The house was heated by a woodstove, which vented smoke through a chimney that curved alarmingly on its path from stove to sky. My parents were of the ilk that seemed forever intent on escaping something, although they never clearly articulated what, exactly, this something might be. They kept goats, drove a VW Beetle, and husbanded extensive vegetable gardens. Hippies are what they were, or maybe back-to-the-landers, although any distinction between the two terms seems less than precise. They were well schooled (Johns Hopkins and Cornell for my father; Grinnell for my mother), but seemed uninterested in the sort of professional-track careers generally assumed to be the outcome of such educations.

Indeed, their "careers," such as they were, seemed purposely built to elude much, if any, recompense. My father worked with words; primarily, he wrote poetry and edited poetry anthologies, and if ever there were a profession less disposed to fiscal remuneration, I'd be curious to know what it is. Finger painting, maybe. My mother kept busy around the homestead and for a time milked cows at a farm up the road. At some point, when I was about 2, my folks sold the farmhouse and the sliver of land on which it sat and built a cabin at the boundary of field and forest, a good quarter-mile off the gravel town road. It was a small cabin, two rooms, really, with a loftlike second floor and a deck on the woods side. It did not have electricity or running water. If you needed to pee, you went outside. If you needed to take a dump, and it was January and 20 below, first you held it, then you held it some more, then you cursed, then you beelined for the outhouse.

I don't remember feeling poor, but I know that we were. I mean, we always had plenty to eat and presents at Christmas and that sort of thing, but the day-in, day-out details of our existence were rooted in poverty. Cars broke and were not immediately fixed; clothes were patched and then, when the patches wore through, patched again. Clearly, it wasn't a grinding sort of poverty, and I suspect it was not entirely dissimilar to Erik's poverty, which is to say that it looked poorer from the outside than it felt on the inside.

My father, in particular, has always been thrifty, and at times downright miserly. Even as he progressed from the realm of poetry to more lucrative pastures, eventually earning a solid middle-class income, he remained the sort of fellow whose happiness is largely disconnected from finance. Instead, he finds his joy in both quiet observations of the world around him and a variety of esoteric pursuits that, beyond their eccentricity, share the singular commonality that they cost almost nothing. Here is my father, carefully balancing a raw egg on its end, a feat of derring-do that demands a long and disciplined nurturing of skill. That, and a mop. There he is, growing monster pumpkins, carefully cultivated orbs of orange flesh that have no purpose but to be admired, before collapsing in on themselves as they decompose into the very soil from which they came. Listen to him as he speaks backwards (sdrawkcab skaeps eh sa mih ot netsil); watch him grow artichokes in central Vermont, a climate wholly unsuited to the task (the horticultural equivalent of downhill skiing in Miami). For a time, he was buying old, unrecognizably crusted and degraded coins on eBay and polishing them at home. This hobby did not seem to last as long as his others, I suspect because it cost too much to keep up.

At the risk of being accused of pop psychology, I can't help but consider my father's backstory and wonder about the bearing it must have had on his view of things relating to money.

My father was born in 1943 and reared alongside his brothers in Montclair, New Jersey. His father, Frederick Hewitt, had had the good fortune to inherit upwards of $5 million from his parents; this was back in the 1920s, when a million bucks was, well, a hell of a lot of money. It still isn't peanuts, of course, but understand that according to the consumer price index, $1 million in 1920 would these days be the equivalent of almost $11 million. Which is to say, my father was born into an exceptionally wealthy family.

This situation did not last for long because over the final years of my grandfather's life (he died when my father was still a boy), he pretty much blew the whole wad. Actually, he blew more than the whole wad, eventually sinking so deeply into debt that his wife was forced to return to work as a nurse, 7 days per week, in order to simply pay the interest on his debt. The stock market and alcohol are reputed to have played starring roles in my grandfather's financial ruination, as was his habit of making unsecured loans to pretty much anyone who asked. Upon his death, each of his three sons received a modest inheritance of $10,000, courtesy of my grandfather's life insurance policy.

Financially speaking, I contend that this represents a fairly profound fall from grace. Psychologically speaking, I contend that a childhood environment of such economic schizophrenia is extremely likely to make an impression of some sort.

In any event, my father spent his modest share of his father's life insurance payout on the old farmhouse and the 170 acres where

I spent the first 6 years of my life. Perhaps this purchase was reflective of a need to convert liquidity and all its attendant risks to what is arguably the most tangible asset one can assume: land. Maybe my father was afraid that if he didn't spend his money on something of durable value, he'd follow his father's lead and spend it on many somethings of less certain worth. Probably he just wanted a piece of land and a roof over his head.

In my 6th year, my parents moved to a small town a few miles outside the state capital of Montpelier where my father had taken a job at the Vermont Arts Council the year before. As it had for so many of their peers, the appeal of hyper-rural, self-subsistence living had worn thin. The subzero forays to the outhouse, and the long walk from where the decrepit VW was parked at road's edge to the small cabin, half-lit by the smoky flames of kerosene lanterns. The isolation and its inevitable companion, loneliness. It is my observation that few can sustain the romanticization of these things, the veneer of which is slowly worn away by realities on the ground. There was nothing dictating my parents' ascetic lifestyle beyond their own sense of how life should be lived, and they would not be the first to refine that sense so that it aligned with indoor plumbing and light switches.

After a year of caretaking a sprawling, decidedly spooky and defunct country inn, my folks bought themselves a house, complete with a pair of eminently flushable toilets (one on each floor!) and a mortgage. By today's standards, the price was laughably low—$55,000 for a well-constructed and fairly new Cape-style home, situated on 3 acres of mixed hardwoods. Back then, the area was strictly working class, rooted in the trades; it has since largely morphed into a bedroom community of white-collar professionals and modestly successful artists. It's not so much left leaning as it is left horizontal, a community of unapologetic liberals with a predilection for natural fibers, organic produce, and NPR–stickered Subaru station wagons.

My awareness of the profound shift in my family's circumstances was every bit as dim as was appropriate for a 6-year-old. I mean, I must have been cognizant of the fact that we no longer had to urinate outdoors, but it's not as if I remember standing goggle-eyed before the toilet. I did not linger at the entrance to every room, flicking the light switch on and off and on again. I suspect my youth kept me from fully grasping the contrast. Kids are nothing if not resilient and accepting, and I have no reason to believe I was any different.

The assumption of a mortgage and the suddenly commodious nature of his surroundings did little to dampen my father's enthusiasm for thrift. Here was a man who would follow his children (my younger sister having been born during our occupation of the rented inn) throughout their new home, darkening lights in their wake. Here was a man who, along with my mother, slept in the living room on a sprung pullout sofa bed for years, rather than spend the money to acquire a more formal arrangement. Here was a man who could stand to waste nothing, not even the lingering heat still trapped in a pan sitting above an extinguished burner: His most famous kitchen creation was "coaster cakes," the half-raw pancakes he "cooked" on a rapidly cooling griddle. To this day, I cannot abide a pancake that is even slightly underdone.

Look, to many, none of these things may seem particularly radical. I know that. There are plenty of kids with similar memories and plenty of parents who are even thriftier, driven either by circumstance or compulsion. I'm not trying to lay claim to anything exceptional; I'm merely framing the rough context for the origins of my personal relationship to money.

I don't want to get too psychoanalytical, but it is hard to ignore the financial aspects of my lineage. A spendthrift grandfather, a thrifty-if-not-downright-cheap father: How might these inform my own relationship to thrift and abundance? One could make an argument for either extreme. Perhaps the wastrel gene would skip a generation, further mutated by rebellion against the paucity of my childhood. Or might the lessons of my grandfather's plight, coupled with the uncomfortable truth that apples rarely fall particularly far from the tree, resonate through the generations?

It seems to have been the latter, although I'm only 40 years old, and there is still ample time to reverse course; after all, my grandfather managed to hold on to his assets until the waning years of his life. The difference is, of course, that I don't have millions of dollars to hold on to. I don't even have tens of thousands of dollars, which is the occasionally discomfiting result of having opted to put my faith in writing as a career path. In this sense my financial destiny has been chosen for me, though it could just as well be argued that I could have chosen a career that would have painted an entirely different financial backdrop. After all, I was offered the educational opportunities that might have made this possible, but I chose not to take them.[6]

Still, my prevailing point remains intact, which is that even before Erik came into my life, I'd embraced a relatively Spartan existence. The story of how we came to acquire our land and build our house is a fine example of this embrace.

My wife, Penny, and I bought our land in 1997, back when I was 26 years old and before Penny became my wife. At the time, we were living in a tent we'd pitched on land belonging to friends, saving our loot, and waiting for the right property to present itself. Although I remember this time with no small degree of fondness, it is only the gift of hindsight that allows me to do so, for the tent was dark and lousy with mold, and I spent much of the summer

---

[6] In the interest of full disclosure, I am a high school dropout, although I did complete two semesters of college after acquiring my GED. In a very real sense, my truncated, atypical educational path has actually enabled me to pursue the career of my choosing, since I was not in a position of student loan repayment and therefore did not have to seek out a high-paying but possibly unfulfilling line of work in order to service this debt.

with a cough that would not relent. We established a rudimentary kitchen of sorts in an old canvas army shelter, but the roof leaked profusely, a defect that was exacerbated by a summer of record-setting rainfall.

Then quite suddenly it wasn't summer (this is generally how it happens in Vermont; one day, you're dripping sweat in your skivvies, the next you're shoveling 2 feet of snow off the driveway), and I was still coughing and we were still in the tent. If the rain had been a certain type of challenge, the snow was another, altogether. Unlike rainwater, it did not run either off or through the roof of our humble dwelling; the threat of our tent collapsing beneath the snow's accumulated weight was a constant companion. We poked at our canvas ceiling with a poplar branch we'd liberated from a nearby tree (ah! Another threat: deadfalls and windblown branches), but we couldn't reach the center of the tent roof. This is to say nothing of the cold, which the thin layer of canvas did little to abate.

This was not the first tent we'd lived in and, frankly, it was an improvement over the sad array of decrepit cabins we'd inhabited over the previous years as part of our savings campaign. At this point, we'd budgeted $100 per month for rent; looking back, I see how brazen and patently absurd this was, and yet, for many years, we paid no more, although it meant inhabiting structures that made the bungalow of my childhood seem downright opulent. Still, we had little choice in the matter, because the income we earned back then came from my part-time job fixing bicycles and writing the occasional newspaper or magazine story, and from Penny's work on a vegetable farm. Between us, we brought home maybe $600 per week, and often, much less.

Still, over the course of about 2 years, we managed to save $15,000, a feat attributable to little more than an extreme tolerance of substandard accommodations and a studied avoidance of anything but the most essential expenditures. To save on gas, and because our car was often disabled, Penny and I both rode our bikes to and from our respective jobs. At the end of her shift, she would fill her backpack and carry home the gnarled, unmarketable carrots and rutabagas, which we would stew with pasta in water that had been hauled from wherever we could find it. The too-frequent result was a sort of "mushy-vegetable-broth-over-linguine" style of cuisine that we generally ate straight from the pot, since washing dishes meant hauling more water.

As mentioned, we did have a car, a little rust-bitten Volkswagen, the mid-1990s equivalent to the Beetle my parents had owned when I was a child, but it was so bereft it lacked a passenger-side rearview mirror. This was not because its mirror had been lost or stolen, but because the friggin' thing had come straight from the factory without one. The car was the epitome of utilitarian transportation, little more than motor, steering wheel, and tires. This explains why it had appealed to my father in the first place, who had driven it until his mechanic had deemed it unsafe, at which point my dear old dad gifted it to us.[7]

Our search for land had proven frustrating. Mostly, this was because our vision and our bank account could not come to terms. The former looked out across acres of rolling fields and verdant forest; we'd plant a garden and some fruit trees, and in the spring, we'd frolic naked through apple blossoms that drifted on the breeze while a small flock of soft-fleeced lambs grazed in a distant meadow. There would be no neighbors to see us, because there would be no neighbors in sight. We'd build a house with our own hands, just the two of us, something small and funky but replete with the luxuries we'd forsaken for so long: Running water. Maybe even hot running water. A bathroom. A roof so

---

[7] This is a joke. I don't think the car was any worse off than when it had left the Volkswagen factory. Which is to say, it was plenty unsafe, but not because of anything my father had done to it.

sturdily constructed no amount of snow could conquer it. Ah, and insulation. Definitely insulation.

That's what we saw. What realtors saw was a pair of scruffy young lovebirds with a mere $15,000.[8] Sure, it was a fortune to us; it was our life's savings, and more money than either of us could ever have imagined laying claim to. We were so stunned by that trio of zeros, it might as well have been $15 million. Except, of course, it wasn't, which explains why we spent a dispiriting summer-and-a-half being dragged across logged-over stubble and cedar-clogged swamps. We were told these parcels had "potential," although precisely how that potential might be realized—and even what that potential might ultimately reveal—remained suspiciously vague.

Our luck changed on a cold and wet October day that foretold the months of cold and wet still to come. When non-Vermonters think of the climactic hardships we must surely endure, they tend to think of deep winter—the frozen realm of January and February, all ice and white and numbed extremities. But I tell you what: The shoulder seasons are much, much harder. At least in January, you know pretty much what to expect. Yes, it's gonna be snowy. Yes, it's gonna be cold. Damn straight, there's going to come a day when you seriously consider chucking it all in and making a beeline for the Mason-Dixon Line as fast as your sorry-ass little VW Fox can take you, watching with glee as the snow-covered landscape disappears in your rearview mirror. But at least you know to expect this.

October, on the other hand, is a reckless, capricious thing. It can be 70 and sunny one day, the sky azure and boundless, the air a soft caress. The first killing frost has come and mercilessly dispatched the insects that find their succor in human blood. But it does not last; it cannot last, and, as one who has passed nearly 40

---

[8]We did, in fact, speak to a bank about preapproval for a mortgage. But upon hearing they were willing to lend us upwards of $100,000, we were frightened into retreat. It was simply too much money for us to fathom, and far too much for us to owe.

Vermont Octobers, I assure you, it will not last. A day later, 2 at the most, and you'll be stuck in a towering drift of autumnal snow. It's not that the weather itself is so bad; rather, it's the schizophrenic, almost psychotic nature of it. It is constantly shifting. There is nothing on which to hang your hat.

By October standards, the day our luck changed was neither bad nor good. Yes, it was cold and wet, but it could have been colder and wetter. And the landscape had a stark beauty to it that the older I get, the more I appreciate. The birches looked like tall bones against the gray of the day, and the state's vaunted maple trees had shed all but the most stubborn of their leaves. The ones that remained were brittle and tarnished orange, but the rain had both softened and brightened them, and from a distance, they looked almost like fireflies against the stolid sky.

We'd found the real estate listing almost by chance, a small advertisement in the back pages of a local newspaper. For months, we'd been ferreting these papers back to our cold, moldy tent, where we'd scan the classifieds by the light of our headlamps. This listing promised 40 acres, with about 10 in pasture. It was set far back off the main road, with a vaguely worded reference to a right-of-way and absolutely no mention of electrical service, which of course meant there was no such thing. Most crucially, it was $30,000, a figure that was particularly resonant, for we knew the banks would issue loans for bare land only with a 50 percent down payment, which was exactly what we had saved. Here, finally, was real potential.

On that cold (but not too cold) and wet (but not too wet) day, we trailed the realtor as he pushed through wild raspberry whips, looking for the rusty barbed wire that marked the boundary lines. His rubber boots left deep impressions in the damp soil. I remember liking the fact that the boundaries were marked this way; it whispered agrarianism, honest toil, and history, and it felt to me as if I could make a life on land that whispered these things. The property sloped gently to the southwest; it was rectangular, topped by the overgrown pasture, which fell into another 30 acres choked with black cherry, fir, maple, poplar, and spruce. There were even a few red oaks, a rarity this far north. Across the valley, we could see the long, low barns of dairy farms and the patchwork of fields rimmed by stone walls and dotted with Ayrshire, Holstein, and Jersey dairy cows. We pretended to listen to the agent's selling points, pretended to be careful, cautious buyers, pretended, even, to be taking notes, but already, we knew. "I love it," I hissed to Penny and she nodded furiously, her eyes as wide as the far mountain views from the height of the land. We made an offer that night.

The bank matched our $15,000, although the interest rate was rapacious: 12 percent. Our good friend Jerry, a fast-talking New Yorker who'd fled the city for rural Vermont with the proceeds from the much-coveted taxi medallions he'd inherited and sold, lent us another 10 grand with which to build a shelter. The interest rate was only slightly less insulting. Jerry was a friend, not a fool, and he charged us 10 percent.

With the loan from Jerry, we built what I euphemistically termed a "hippie shack." It was 16 feet by 32 feet; concrete piers for a foundation; a loft we accessed via an aluminum ladder; and, for the first year and a half or so, no running water, although we did have a well drilled, upon which we installed a hydrant. Dishes and bathing were done at the base of this hydrant with great rapidity, and creative use of profanity. Still, it was a giant leap from the haul-water-in-the-backseat-of-the-car-to-our-canvas-tent-kitchen arrangement, and we tried not to be ungrateful. Another friend gifted us 3 weeks of labor as a wedding present; it was just enough to get the shell up and keep the rain off our heads.

Within 3 years, we'd repaid Jerry's loan and convinced a different bank to lend us $50,000. This was no small feat because the money was intended for the construction of a home that would be situated at the end of a 1,300-foot driveway, and the home would not be—nor would it ever be—connected to the electrical grid. Banks aren't really down with alt energy, but at this bank there was a family connection from way back, and he called in a favor or two and badabing, badaboom, we had our money. Or credit. Or whatever you want to call it. I remember being slightly stunned by it all; only a few years before, I could hardly imagine being the master of $15,000, and here I was in possession of more than three times as much. I didn't really think about where the money had come from; like most people, I had a vague notion that the bank had lent me 50 grand of its money. The truth, of course, is that they had simply assigned numbers to my account. There was no money, or at least there wasn't until I spent it.[9]

Via this odd arrangement, we jacked up the hippie shack and poured a real foundation under it, along with a basement for an addition that by itself was larger than the original structure. I remember well the day this happened, for I was on the whipping end of a particularly tight writing deadline and could not afford to miss a day of work just because my house (and therefore, my office, which consisted of a desk wedged into a corner of the loft) was about to get a few feet closer to the sun.

"Do you think it'd be alright if I stay in the house while yer liftin' it?" I asked Gary, assuming the regional dialect in hopes of connecting with the fellow on a Vermonter-to-Vermonter basis, and thus earning his approval to remain on task. Gary was the contractor we'd hired to lift the house, which demanded both exceptional delicacy and brute force, a pairing of qualities that seems dichotomous but which in rural Vermont is actually quite common.

I'd come to like Gary quite a bit. But I liked him even more when he rubbed his stubbled chin thoughtfully and cast a glance at the cabin, which was to be raised a total of 4 feet. Already, not yet having been moved a single inch, the cabin looked disturbingly vulnerable with its foundation piers removed and replaced by a

---

[9] Much more on this later.

latticework of cribbing, as if the damn thing was sitting on a bed of pick-up sticks. Gary looked at me, then back to the cabin, as if making a mental calculation regarding my tolerance for risk and his responsibility not to kill me. Finally, he broke into a grin: "Can't see how it could hurt."

My desk was situated at a window that looked out the northern gable end of our little home, and it was there I sat, typing away, as the house slowly rose beneath me. It felt as if I was levitating, and it is not a sensation I will ever forget. Every so often, the cabin would sway from side to side, like a cradle. And yes, I hit my deadline.

With our house in the air and our loan approved, we bought materials: Towering stacks of lumber and roofing and drywall. Windows. Doors. I took the summer off from the bike shop, and Penny starting taking 3-day weekends. Our friend Bob, a skilled carpenter possessing a torso that has always reminded me of a beer keg, came every weekend with a truck full of tools and a lifetime of experience warehoused in his stocky frame. Our energy and enthusiasm seemed boundless, and by the end of the summer, our shack had become a house. It wasn't finished, of course, but if you stood back far enough and squinted, you could sort of imagine what it would look like with siding.

That winter, our first child was born, a boy, and we named him Finlay. Appropriately enough, Penny went into labor at the lumberyard, where she was picking out shower tiles.[10] "I just want

---

[10] By now you might reasonably be wondering where one meets the sort of woman who is content to inhabit a tent in order to save money toward land, and who goes into labor with her first child at a lumberyard. In short, Penny and I met on the island of Martha's Vineyard, where I had gone to spend a winter doing construction and where she was doing odd jobs. We met on a job site on a typically raw February day, when she showed up at 7:00 a.m. on her bicycle to dig a trench for the sprinkler system. It was raining and about 40°F and, furthermore, she had a shovel lashed to her bike with frayed rope. What kind of woman rode her bicycle in the near-freezing rain on an early February morning to dig a ditch for $12 per hour? Only one kind: the kind I wanted to get to know a bit better.

to have the shower finished before the baby comes," she'd told me, which would have worked out fine if Fin had been oh, about 3 *months* late. As it turned out, our place was in such a state of incompleteness that when the midwife arrived to assist us with a homebirth, she swiveled her head with evident distaste and said, "You've got a long way to go." And this was *after* I'd moved the miter and table saws to the basement to better facilitate the birthing process. She then parked herself in a rocking chair set in the doorway of the bedroom and promptly began to snore. I never had liked her much; I liked her even less after that.

Fin's arrival slowed our progress for a few weeks, but frankly, not as much as I'd expected. The little duffer slept remarkably well, and we suffered little of the fatigue that tends to afflict first-time parents. By the next summer, our house was finished enough that the bank converted our construction loan to a regular mortgage, which dropped our interest rate from 9 percent to a less draconian 6 percent.

For the next 6 or 7 years, we did everything in our power to pay off our mortgage, and to the extent I can point to a specific time when my aversion to debt became a life-altering force, this is it. I could not *stand* having that debt; it felt burdensome beyond all reason, like a whole-body flu I couldn't shake. Intellectually, I grasped that it was a relatively modest sum (in addition to the $50K, we had another 10 grand or so that we revolved through a series of low-interest credit card offers, this being the era of seemingly boundless offers for 12 months at zero percent), and that our payments were well within our means. By this time, my writing career had begun to bring in enough cash that we felt downright flush. I hadn't yet reached the heady heights of the $35,000 years, but in comparison to my bike shop wages, which hovered around 8 bucks an hour, we were walkin' in tall cotton. I've come to understand that monetary affluence is largely a condition of comparison, and by the standards of my modest expectations, forged by both my childhood and the earlier years of my working life, we were loaded. We could well afford to service our measly $370 mortgage payment.

Actually, we could afford *more*, so we obsessively began making double and sometimes even triple payments. This was not all my doing, obviously, and I should mention Penny's role in all this. She was, as much, if not more so than I, the one pushing for rapid retirement of our debt. And she was, inarguably more so than I, willing to do whatever it took to make this happen. This was a period of unrelenting paucity and patience because, as it turns out, $50,000 isn't really that much with which to raise a house, even if you're supplying the bulk of the blood, sweat, and tears. By the time we had the roof screwed down and the windows installed, our pile of money/credit had evaporated, and any "luxuries" were eschewed in favor of rapid repayment. Kitchen cabinets? *Who needs 'em!* A finished floor in the living room? *Hold yer horses, boy: Not until the loan's paid off!*[11]

Was there any rational reason to fight so frenetically against our burden of debt? Remember, this was the late '90s, in the heady days of the Internet bubble. I mean, did the word "austerity" even exist back then? Probably, but if so, only in dictionaries and the specialized vocabularies of economists. During that period, Erik Gillard was but a child, really, not yet able to vote or buy a bottle of beer. Oh sure, there was the usual assortment of beard-toting anticapitalist curmudgeons scattered about, grumbling about globalization, corporatism, and mindless consumerism. But there's no denying that the prevailing national mood was one of delighted optimism and giddy anticipation for a future that seemed, if anything, brighter than the present. Really, how else to explain the coincident rise of the sport utility vehicle, the model names of

---

[11] I feel compelled to point out that the loan has since been retired, and we *still* don't have a finished floor in the living room.

which bespoke a yearning to push with feckless abandon into the 21st century: Explorer. Navigator. Blazer. Pathfinder.

I'm not suggesting it wasn't rational to absolve ourselves of debt; I'm only noting that there was little in the broader culture of the day that presented it as a sensible choice. Nor can I lay claim to any sort of intellectualized ethos in my relationship to debt. Our quest was not part of a quiet protest; we weren't disavowing usury, or attempting to drop out of the capitalist system. Hell, I *liked* making and having money, and I was excited to realize that I might actually achieve "middleclassdom," a socioeconomic status I'd long assumed would always prove elusive.

Therefore, to explain my acute aversion to debt, I can only return to the sense of near dread I felt every time our monthly mortgage reminder arrived at our little community post office. I've long had the habit of peeking through the small window of our mailbox door to see what clues I might discern from that limited vantage point. A child's game, I know, but hey: We all need occasional reminders not to take life so damn seriously.

Now, it may have helped that I knew when, give or take a day or two, our mortgage slip was due to arrive each month (always on or around the 15th), but I never failed to identify the bank's distinct cream-colored envelope, even before I saw the return address offset against the smooth paper. This positive identification was accompanied by an acute sense of physical and emotional discontent. What I felt was not quite nausea, and not quite depression, but something subtler. A distinct *unease* if you will, which lasted for as long as it took me to become distracted by more pressing concerns.

This sensation was particularly acute during the early years of repayment, when each check I sent did little to affect the totality of our debt load. I mean, even if I made a double payment, we were still looking at a $700 reduction. Now, 700 bucks ain't nothing, but in the context of 50 large, it's not a hell of a lot, and the difference between owing the bank $50,000 and $49,300 is hardly worth mentioning. Besides which, once interest was factored into the equation, a $700 payment only reduced our principal by a measly 200 bucks, if that. Things started to turn near the end of our payoff when, knowing we'd dipped into four-digit territory, my lingering feelings of dread mingled with something that felt almost like anticipation. At this point, each payment had a measurable impact on the remaining total. Seven hundred dollars from $5,000 feels like real progress, like a direct blow to the debt shackles that bind: *Take that, sucka!*

The closest I can come to a logical explanation for our obsession is this: I am fearful that I will someday find myself obliged to earn money at a job I don't like in order to make good on the debt I've accrued. It occurred to me fairly early on in my adult life that the best and easiest place to allay my fear is at the outset of that treadmill. No debt = no need to service debt = not having to work to service the debt. It was math so basic, even I could understand it.

The upshot to all of this is that by the time my 37th birthday arrived, I inhabited a home that belonged entirely to Penny and me. The bank no longer had any stake in our house and land; so long as we kept up with our annual property taxes, no one could pile our belongings on the curb and kick us into the street. I would like to report that this marked a profound shift in our lives, but the truth is that things carried on pretty much as they had before. Because our mortgage payment had been entirely manageable, the sense of freedom realized by absolving ourselves of it was not as acute as we anticipated it might have been. Still, I can't deny the satisfaction derived from dropping that last payment into the "outgoing" slot at the post office. That thin envelope carried more than a check and the stub from our payment reminder; it carried the not-insignificant weight of my debt-related obsession, and I knew that, barring some unforeseen turn of events, I would never again carry debt. Admittedly, that was only 4 years ago, so my fidelity to that pledge hasn't yet had terribly many opportunities to be tested. But it also hasn't failed me.

Look, I get it: The decision to eschew debt is an enormous luxury, afforded by no small amount of luck and good timing. The most obvious is the simple fact that we purchased our land before the onslaught of the real estate bubble. Even now, with that bubble in the latter stages of deflation, we couldn't touch a comparable piece of property for anything close to what we paid. Score one for right place, right time. And then there were the less obvious factors from which we benefited: my paternal ancestors' uncommon relationship to money, as well as the evolution of our skills relating to the pragmatic. Having dabbled in the trades, we possessed the rough knowledge necessary to put a roof over our heads, and what we didn't know, we could glean from our network of friends, a benefit that is part and parcel of a less tangible but no less crucial factor in our successful quest to absolve ourselves of debt: We'd chosen to make a life in a region that does not revere excess. I'm generalizing, of course, but broadly speaking, northern Vermont is not a keep-up-with-the-Joneses sort of place. Indeed, at times it can seem as if overt displays of monetary and asset affluence are discouraged, and I think it seems this way because, in fact, they are. The rural hollows of my home state are imbued with a reverence for thrift and resourcefulness; it's a place where people hunt not so much for sport as for food, and where the rust holes in our pickups are patched with duct tape and cast-off scraps of metal roofing. As a friend who moved to the region from the Dallas–Fort Worth area told me, "You have no idea what it's like out there. You have no idea what the expectations are." By "out there," I understood that he meant not merely DFW, but America writ large. By "expectations," I understood that he was speaking of the unspoken social pressure to maintain appearances. He'd come from a place where tape was for taping, and roofing was for roofing, and that "place" was the America inhabited by the overwhelming majority of her people.

There's an obvious offshoot to the resourcefulness imbedded in my community: the acquisition of skills. More specifically, I'm speaking of the skills relating to the pragmatic and analog particulars of human existence in the 21st century, so many of which have been surrendered to the assumption that the economy of the future is one in which the majority will delegate the messier, sweatier essentials to either the unwashed minority or, if the techno-copians are to be believed, the manufactured technology that will result in the end of blisters and Band-Aids. Culturally speaking, the capacity to provide for ourselves the fundamentals required for simple survival has eroded over time, along a trajectory that maintains an inverse relationship to monetary affluence. This is presumed to represent an increased "standard of living," and seems rooted in the assumption that writing video game code and managing hedge funds are more financially viable and culturally laudable occupations than, say, building houses or growing food.

In certain outposts of our nation, including the outpost where we make our home, these assumptions have had trouble gaining traction. Which is to say that we are surrounded by people who know how to make things. And by "things," I mean things you can hold, things you can eat, and things you can sleep in. I mean things that embody a physical form, that provide the building blocks of the essentials on which we all ultimately depend. Food and shelter are the most obvious, but they extend up the hierarchy of needs and wants and on into the realm of the not-strictly-essential-but-awfully-damn-nice-to-have: musical instruments, tools, and furniture are just a few that come to mind. I don't mean to suggest that expertise in the trades is unique to rural Vermont, but this is undeniably a region occupied by more than its share of producers.

The point is that much as money begets money, I have come to understand thrift begets thrift. And it does this, at least in part, because the pursuit of thrift demands a type of resourcefulness that almost inevitably leads to the quest for, and acquisition of, more skills. And as one becomes connected to the network of people who rely on these skills, one becomes exposed to an ever-broader array of talents and flat-out cleverness, allowing one to further elude monetary abundance. This is not so surprising, really. Still, we tend to think of opportunity resulting primarily from a relentless climb up the socioeconomic ladder. It's interesting to me to consider the ways in which climbing down creates its own opportunities.

Therefore, and as my friend from Texas astutely points out, it has been no small advantage to have been raised in a community imbued with both a lack of interest in financial excess and the skills necessary to maintain that lack of interest. In other words, I was privileged to be *socialized* to thrift and resourcefulness, and to be born into a network of capable people to call upon when my own skills fall short, as they so often do. It is no exaggeration to say that without this network, it is extremely unlikely we could have built a 2,200-square-foot home for $50,000. This truth inevitably leads me to the conclusion that without this network, it is extremely unlikely we could have bought our way out of debt before either of us hit 40. Or even 50.

Yet, for all of this, it is astonishing to consider the extent to which I have allowed my sense of affluence to be dictated by financial circumstances. I describe my years as "good" or "bad," with "good" or "bad" referring strictly to my income, as if all the other forces in my life are secondary. It is amazing to consider how much I have given myself over to the cultural mythology of money-is-wealth, wringing my hands over retirement funds and savings accounts that seem ever inadequate, even as my family's day-to-day needs and wants are met, time and time again. I take jobs strictly for the money, even when the money meets no immediate or even medium-term need. In other words, I find myself working more to earn for no other reason that to accumulate, to strengthen my so-called safety net, even as doing so pulls me out of the flow of my life and into the choppy current of money.

It is probably clear by now that, speaking strictly in financial terms, we are not wealthy. But that's hardly the point. The point is that even I, with my innate aversion to debt and immersion in a proud culture of "use it up, wear it out, make it do, or do without," have succumbed. I have begun to believe that this acquiescence is in large part responsible for my failure to recognize the true wealth that surrounds me. And what it is really worth.

[CHAPTER SIX]

In which I consider matters of appropriate scale, industrialism, embedded energy, the creation of money, and the commodification of the natural world. Oh, and rocks. Those, too.

FOLLOWING MY morel hunt with Breakfast and Erik, only a few weeks of spring remained. They passed quickly, as Vermont spring weeks are wont to do. Every few days, after tending to farm chores, I struck out from my home and allowed myself to be swallowed by the dense forest that extends from our property to the north and west. Despite deliberate searching at the base of numerous dead elm and apple trees, I found no more morels.

At first, this was disappointing; my share of the take from my excursion with Breakfast and Erik had lasted for exactly two meals. To cook the mushrooms, I melted generous portions of sweet butter in a pan and dropped the morels into the melted fat to sizzle and shrivel as the heat forced moisture from their cells. I'd sliced them thin and diagonally, for no other reason than this was how I'd seen good cooks slice things, and they cooked quickly, filling the air with an immersive aroma that was both earthy and fruity. They came out of the pan hot, glistening, and shriveled, and even when cooked, they somehow exuded a pleasing wildness. My family ate them bare-handed, licking warm butter and the essence of mushroom from our fingers.

The boys clamored for more mushrooms; to appease them, I learned to identify other species of fungi in the damp softwood stands to the north of our home, where golden chanterelles, spiny hedgehogs, and barrel-capped boletes proliferated. It became rare for me to return home with a less-than-full baseball cap, and on occasion I was even forced to fashion a satchel from my T-shirt, although I never achieved Erik's sanguinity in the face of the blackflies. Once, when battling a particularly bloodthirsty swarm of the little buzzing bastards, I dumped an entire shirt-load onto the forest floor. After that, I carried a paper bag for my stash, although, I had to admit, it lacked panache.

In any case, I reveled in my newfound foraging skills. The notion that I could feed my family simply by slipping into the woods for an hour or two was immensely pleasing to me; it struck a primeval chord that seemed to resonate in some ancient part of me I hadn't even known existed. One of the things I've always loved about growing food is that it feels *real*. When I push my hands into the cool soil to unearth a fist-sized potato that I planted only months ago from the previous year's seed stock, I am unearthing one of the most essential and tangible assets known to humanity: food. And by having sown, tended, and harvested the crop myself, I am free of the layers of commerce that generally mediate these exchanges in contemporary America. The only commerce—if you want to call it that—is between the soil, the spud, and me.

Still, there was something about foraging that both expanded and elevated this sense of freedom. There was no meddling with nature's process; no soil to be turned, no weeds to be pulled, no fat potato beetles to be popped between the thumb and forefinger. There was only the forest and I, and as I walked beneath the lush canopy of trees, I felt at once tuned in and relaxed in a way that eludes me during my workaday tasks. Everything was acute and vibrant: colors, smells, the calls of birds, the scurrying of squirrels, and even the sensation of my feet pressing into the soft bed of needles and leaves. And what of that sense of the ancient, that primeval chord that rang quietly but clearly every time I focused my vision on the land, in search of nourishment? It was subtle, and so deeply historical I couldn't put a finger on its origins, but I wondered if perhaps it represented the true foundation of my humanity; the millennia of hunting and gathering that preceded me. We tend to think of agriculture as being the foundation on which our societies are built, but of course cultivated crops have been around for only a fraction of human history. The general anthropological consensus is that we have practiced agriculture for a mere 5 percent of our existence.

Some days I did not gather mushrooms but instead simply wandered, rambling aimlessly across the land. It was startling to realize how little I knew about my surroundings, how little time I'd allowed myself to get to know the land to which we had held title for 15 years. I roamed up, down, and across our property, sometimes following old skidder paths, sometimes pushing through the thorny underbrush, my hands raised in a protective "x" across my face.

This is how I came to find the old maple sugarhouse, barely a quarter-mile from our front door. It was tucked into an impressive stand of fir; the trees pushed 100 or more feet into the sky, and some measured a full 2 feet across at their base. Little remained of the original structure but its foundation stones and the sugaring rig, which was rusted and listing, slowly returning to the rich forest soil. The first time I saw the dilapidated rig, out the corner of one eye, I was startled. From a distance, it looked like the flesh-stripped bones of a great beast. A dozen or so feet away, an old sugaring pan lay half buried in decades of accumulated forest duff.

There was something about the foundation that drew me to it, although I can't say exactly what that something was. I began to visit it often, usually in the early morning. I'd stroll down through the dew-wet grass of our meadow, and then enter the cool sanctuary of the trees, before perching myself on one of the stones, a smooth, flat wedge of basalt that was always cool to the touch, no matter the weather. There was something unshakable in the integrity of those rocks, which I knew had been pulled there by the hoofed power of some loyal beast, and then stacked by hand. Sitting atop the foundation, I imagined the draft horses, dust and chaff stuck to a sheen of sweat, and I considered their masters, bent to the task of arranging the stones into their final resting places. Looking up, I could almost see the wooden structure that had long since fallen away and been consumed by the forest, and I marveled at the toil of it all: the toothed saw blade's back-and-forth, back-and-forth; the honed and oiled bit of the axe rising and falling, again and again and again; and the buckets of sap heavy and sloshing, 40 or more gallons to make just 1 of syrup, each gallon of sap weighing better than 8 pounds, and most of it to be boiled away, the water content rising from the sugarhouse and drifting into the air as if it were nothing at all.[12]

---

[12] So now you know why maple syrup typically fetches $50 or more per gallon; although modern sugaring technology has made the process less labor intensive, it still consumes copious amounts of time and energy.

I knew it was for the syrup—or perhaps more precisely, for the money the syrup would bring—that someone had once gathered and arranged those hundreds of stones. It had been the same someone who, perhaps with the assistance of family and neighbors, then felled the trees and shaped them, first singly and then collectively, into a building; who cut and piled the sugaring wood; who hung the empty buckets and regathered them, full to the brim with sap; who stoked the fire in the big rig; and who sat up late as steam rose high into the night sky. What might they have been thinking? Of the morning chores that would come all too soon? Of what they'd buy with the syrup money and how that money might ease some of the burdens of their life? Surely they wondered over the weather, hoping for another sap run or two before the maples budded out and the season ended as abruptly as it had begun.

It was the scale of the sugarhouse that suggested to me that it had been constructed primarily for the income it would provide. The question, of course, is what happened? Why wasn't it still standing, and why couldn't I even find the big sugar maples that would have been essential to the viability of such an operation? Oh sure, a handful of sugar maples still stood scattered about, graceful giants that had seen generations of humans born and then, a lifetime later, lowered into the ground. But no matter how generous these few trees might have been, they could never have kept that evaporator pan full. I knew that once there had been dozens, if not hundreds, more maples, but they were long gone, harvested for firewood or high-grade lumber. The money would have likely been good, or at least good enough that the only remaining evidence of their existence was the large hummocks that dotted the forest floor like little graves.

Of course, it's impossible to know with certainty why the trees and the sugarhouse were gone—a death in the family, a change of ownership, a fire, a simple shift in interests—but it is not hard to imagine a plausible scenario, if for no other reason than that the condition of its remnants suggests it was built prior to the widespread adoption of internal combustion technology. To anyone alive today, the extreme concentration of energy fossil fuels provide, and the ever-increasing scale of industry they enable, does not seem an anomaly. No matter how much we might gripe about rising gas prices, the fact is, we have all been born and raised in an era of cheap, abundant, and accessible energy. It is worthwhile to consider that the energy contained in a single barrel of oil is roughly equivalent to 11 *years* of physical labor for a healthy adult man. The United States consumes approximately 19 million barrels of oil each and every day, which means that every 24 hours we consume the equivalent of 209 million years of one person's physical labor.

The industrial capacity enabled by this incredible concentration of toil and the shifts in manufacturing process that exploited this capacity created a tidal wave of goods. Economy of scale and efficiency were hallmarks of this period, which is perhaps best exemplified by Henry Ford's invention in 1910 of a "line production system" for the assembly of his company's automobiles. Prior to instituting this system, the average time required to assemble a single chassis was 12 hours and 28 minutes; within only 4 years, Ford had cut that to a mere 1 hour and 33 minutes. These sorts of "gains" played out again and again, across all industrial boundaries, creating a glut of manufactured products in search of a home.

To help absorb that glut, manufacturers turned to the advertising industry for help with marketing their products, most aggressively to the very people who produced them. In 1918, total gross magazine advertising revenue was $58.5 million; by 1920, the total had reached $129.5 million. But the numbers tell only half the story, because this was a period that saw the advent of emotion-based marketing designed to exploit base desires for social status and simple acceptance. "The utilitarian value of a product or the traditional notion of mechanical quality were no longer sufficient inducements to move merchandise at the necessary rate and volume required by mass production," writes Stewart Ewen in his book *Captains of Consciousness*, which chronicles the rise of mass production and industry's attempts to capitalize on it. "The creation of 'fancied need' was crucial to the modern advertiser. The transcendence of traditional consumer markets and buying habits required people to buy, not to satisfy their own fundamental needs, but rather to satisfy the real, historic needs of capitalist productive machinery." In other words, it's not about what *you* need; it's about what industry needs you to *think* you need.

Of course, the era of oil, the increasing capacity of industry, and the cleverly worded copy of advertising agencies are not the sole causes of the ever-widening divide between nature and us. Nor do they fully explain how it is that we have arrived at a hollow and ultimately detrimental definition of wealth. And they do not reveal why we have willingly squandered so much of our true prosperity in our scramble to accumulate money and physical assets. They are certainly factors in all of these conditions, and their contributions in these regards have been generous. But there is an underlying factor that drives both industry and fossil fuel consumption in an unrelenting skyward trajectory, and does so by design. Of course, I'm speaking of our monetary system.

It is telling that I feel compelled to interject at this point, lest I risk losing your attention. Because let's be honest: The phrase "monetary system" (along with its sibling "monetary policy") carries the burden of being one of the least exciting pair of words ever to be unleashed upon the innocent people of this nation. What would you do if you were at a party and the fellow next to you started babbling about "monetary policy"? Yeah, I'd probably feel the sudden need to visit the restroom too. Or at the very least, get another drink.

But the fact that relatively few people are cognizant of even the most basic aspects of contemporary monetary policy is unfortunate given the critical role money plays in modern society and the ways in which that role is defined by the policies behind it, which often seem to have been engineered to monetize and commodify almost every aspect of our well-being. And not inconsequently, separate us from the foundation of holistic wealth.

It is often said that contemporary monetary policy is convoluted and arcane, perhaps even by design. Henry Ford, the very same man who revolutionized automobile production, is famous for having said, "It is well enough that people of the nation do not understand our banking and monetary system, for if they did, I believe there would be a revolution before tomorrow morning."[13] Many have offered Ford's quote as evidence that our monetary system is *intentionally* complex, engineered for obfuscation and outright confusion. This may be so, and there's little question that understanding the minutia of money is an exhausting proposal.[14]

In one sense, Henry Ford and the multitudes of others who claim that our money system is complicated beyond the point of reason and basic comprehension are exactly right. But in another sense, they're exactly wrong, because there is one core truth to both our money and its design that tells you pretty much everything you truly need to know about it. This truth is incredibly

---

[13] Somewhat less famously, he also said, "If money is your hope for independence you will never have it. The only real security that a man will have in this world is a reserve of knowledge, experience, and ability."

[14] If for some reason you find yourself drawn to the history and byzantine particulars of US monetary policy, I am happy to recommend a trio of books that address the subject in detail: *The Web of Debt*, by Ellen Hodgson Brown; *Debt: The First 5,000 Years*, by David Graeber; and *The Lost Science of Money*, by Stephen Zarlenga. All three are highly readable, or at least as readable as monetary policy writing is likely to ever get.

simple, so much so that it can be summed up in precisely three words: Money is debt. It is literally *loaned into existence.*

For those of you who are quite justifiably experiencing symptoms of acute disbelief, I want you to know I understand that it sounds absurd and that not so long ago, I struggled mightily with this concept. And for good reason, I believe. After all, we have come to view money as being the very antithesis of debt; you either have money, or you're in debt.[15] So how could they possibly be one and the same?

The idea that money is debt works on levels both literal and metaphoric; my interest here is strictly literal, in no small part because I've already hinted at the metaphoric in previous chapters. If, as I have contended, money is at its core a representation of natural resources and if, as is widely acknowledged, many of the natural resources represented by money are either nonrenewable or so slowly renewable that they will effectively run dry before our need for them does, then it's no stretch to say that we are borrowing these resources from our future. And that the money we exchange as representation of these resources is therefore a debt we owe to our future selves and those who will follow.

But that does little to explain the self-generating nature of money and how that generation is entirely reliant on the continued expansion of debt. To help explain this dynamic, I'm going to return to 1913, the year the Federal Reserve Act was enacted, establishing the very same Federal Reserve that has played such a pivotal role in recent economic events.

The Federal Reserve is popularly understood to be a branch of the federal government, which it emphatically is not. Although the Fed chairman (as of this writing, Ben Bernanke) is appointed by

---

[15] Of course, there is a middle ground, whereby you have neither money, nor debt. But given that most of us use money to secure the essentials of our day-to-day existence, it's pretty hard to exist in these conditions: We need to either accumulate money or go into debt to procure necessities.

the president, the reserve actually consists of a consortium of privately owned banks, including Citibank and J.P. Morgan Chase, that essentially operate with no governmental oversight. The purpose of the Federal Reserve is multifaceted, but its primary raison d'être is the management of our nation's money supply, which it accomplishes through a variety of mechanisms, all of which fall under the umbrella of "monetary policy," which ranks right up there with "money system" in the quest to be Wonkiest Term Ever.

Of these mechanisms, the one that concerns us most is the actual creation of money, which for the purposes of our discussion is understood to include physical currency and debt. The somewhat surprising truth is that the bills in your pocket and the so-called money in your bank account do not exist at the behest of the United States government, as is commonly believed; rather, they were called into being via a convoluted process that defies logic.

Roughly, here's how it works. The Fed is, among other things, a large-scale dealer in government-backed securities—bonds, basically—which it purchases from the US Treasury and then lends to banks through what is known as open market operations. Interestingly—and this is key to understanding how the system works—when the Fed purchases a bond, it counts the bond not as a liability, but as an *asset*, even though it has not been paid in full (or even in part) for the bond. The apt analogy, I suppose, would be if you extended a loan to a friend and, under the assumption that your friend is trustworthy and solvent enough to repay the loan, counted the pending repayment as an asset. As in: "Bubba owes me a hundred bucks, so I have a hundred bucks."

To my way of thinking, this sort of accounting conveniently ignores two key factors. First, the money paid out, which itself had to come from somewhere, and leaves that somewhere a bit poorer; second, the possibility, however remote, that Bubba is going to take your money and split for Jamaica, where he will spend the rest of his days sprawled on a beach consuming enormous quantities of rum, which helps explain why he's totally forgotten about his debt to you.

To be fair, there's some historical precedence supporting the assumption that the US government will make good on its obligation. So it's not as if the Fed is playing the slots. But it gets weirder. Much weirder. Because the Fed now holds this "asset" (which arguably is really a liability), it can create a liability (this time, inarguably so) against the bond purchased from the Treasury. And this liability is created in the form of a check, which it writes to the Treasury in payment for the bond. There is no "money" to cover this check, only the "asset" of the bond it just purchased with the check written against it. In other words, in order to loan a hundred clams to your steadfast buddy Bubba, you purchased a bond from him, and then wrote him a check for the amount of the bond. That's all logical enough, if somewhat convoluted. Here's the real piece of magic: The money you used to purchase Bubba's bond did not come from your savings, but rather from the assets you assume you'll have when Bubba repays the debt. Talk about "creative accounting."

The Fed also lends its so-called assets to banks at the federal funds target rate, which is set by the Fed in reaction to prevailing economic conditions. Generally, if the economy is roaring, the Fed raises the rate to keep growth in check; if it's in the doldrums, the rate is lowered. This rather depressingly explains why the rate has been virtually zero for an extended period of time.

Still, none of this explains how most of the money in our economy is created, and it doesn't fully explain why money is, quite literally, debt. To understand that, you have to understand what happens at the level of individual banks, which are allowed to leverage their reserves, some of which were originally created through the strange arrangement outlined above, through a process known as fractional reserve lending.

Essentially, any money coming into commercial banks, whether from checks cashed by government employees, or assets transferred from the Federal Reserve, or interest income, is listed as a reserve. These are "assets" that the bank actually has, no matter how dubious their origin. But here's the kicker: Banks are allowed to lend nine times more money than they have on reserve. In other words, if a bank holds $100 on reserve, it can lend out $900. Of course, it can charge interest on these loans, and you better bet it's going to be a significantly higher rate than it's paying the Fed. Here's a rhetorical question to make my point: When was the last time your bank offered you a loan at 0.25 percent, which is the current federal funds target rate?

What happens to the repaid loans? Naturally, they are added to the bank's reserves, further expanding the base against which the bank can lend against at a rate of 900 percent. You can see how this might seem like a pretty plum gig for the banks, which are backstopped by the Fed and are doing quite well playing the spread between the interest rate they are charged by the Fed and the interest rate you and I are paying the bank. You can see how this might get a wee bit out of control.

You can also see what I mean when I say "money is debt" because money is, very literally, *loaned* into existence, and not just at a Federal level. It happens every time you or I borrow to buy a car, or a boat, or a house, or whatever. *The money we borrow does not exist until we borrow it.*[16] *It's the same for Bubba, as it is for the federal government, as it is for you and me. The "money" is actually written into existence at the loan origination, to be returned to the bank with interest*, allowing them to expand their reserve base and thus extend more loans to create more so-called money. This helps

---

[16] Okay, so maybe 10 percent of it does, assuming the bank is abiding by the regulations governing its mandated reserves, which is itself a fairly large assumption.

explain why the money supply is always expanding and must always be allowed to do so, because otherwise, the interest accrued by all outstanding loans could not be paid.[17]

But the larger point, I believe, is that while the credit used to purchase an item is simply created out of thin air, the actual item is a product of the real world. At its core, it is a representation of extracted natural resources and the toil involved in both extracting those resources and producing the item. It is a representation—though largely unacknowledged—of the environmental and, too often, the humanitarian toll inherent in the process of resource extraction and the industrial manufacturing it enables. We have, in essence, engineered a system that creates limitless purchasing power against a limited resource base. It may not always feel this way, particularly given the ever-rising wealth and income imbalances in 21st-century America (which is itself a direct result of monetary policy and system design). But of course it matters not who holds the money; it matters not who demands all those resources. It only matters that it happens.

If, as I did, you are struggling to clear this conceptual hurdle, consider the very emblem of American prosperity and contentedness (indeed, the very emblem—however diminished in size and scope—of Erik's prosperity and contentedness): the home. To own a house has become part and parcel of the American Dream, a goal so promoted and deemed so worthy that we willingly—gratefully, even—assume an enormous debt burden in order to achieve it. There are few of us who acquire a home without borrowing; in contemporary America, this is assumed to be a 30-year loan,

---

[17] Actually, this is not strictly true: If the lending institution recycled interest income back into the economy via spending, it is conceivably possible that paid loan interest could be made available to be earned by borrowers, thus enabling them to repay future loans. But most financial institutions (not to mention most individuals and corporations) don't recycle their profits; they invest them, which only exacerbates the situation, since those investments seek a monetary gain.

although it's interesting to consider that there's little historical precedence for such lengthy repayment schedules. As a matter fact, prior to the Depression–era New Deal, which included the National Housing Act of 1934, most home loans were granted on 5- or 10-year terms. By extending the term of the typical mortgage, the Roosevelt administration hoped to sow the seeds of a home ownership boom, which it saw as essential for pulling the economy out of its doldrums.

In any event, the default assumption in 21st-century America is that if one is to buy or build a home, one will be borrowing a fairly hefty chunk of dough. At the time of this writing, the national median home price was a bit over $200,000. Let's assume a quaintly responsible 20 percent down payment, which means the borrower is staring down the fine print of a $160,000 loan. Let's assume further that the bank is abiding by reserve standards; as such it need hold only $16,000 of the loan total. The remainder—$144,000—comes from, well, *nowhere.*

Accepting this reality requires a pretty profound shift in our cultural assumptions. When we borrow money, we imagine the lender transferring its assets to us, based on the promise that we will pay it back, with interest, to accommodate the assumption of rising prices, devalued currency, or (as is generally the case) both. It is difficult to picture it any other way; it is even more difficult to grasp the simple fact that prior to our borrowing it, *the money didn't exist.* There is no "transfer" of funds; there is only an accounting entry that amounts to an exchange of promises. The bank promises the money to us, and ultimately to the seller, while we promise to repay the loan, or forfeit the house.

The question that begs asking is: What does it matter? After all, this is a voluntary arrangement, and at face value, it would seem that everyone gets precisely what he or she wants. Sure, we might gripe about the terms, or moan about the convoluted and cumbersome process, but ultimately the buyer gets the house, the seller gets the increase in bank credit, which it has been conditioned to think of as money, and the bank gets to collect interest, on top of the original principal.

This would all amount to a small, contented circle of commerce, if not for one fact: *The house is real.* This might seem an absurdly obvious statement, but given the fictitious nature of the medium (I'm not sure I'm comfortable even using the word "money" anymore) used to purchase and construct the home, it's a statement that bears examination. Consider the constituent parts of the house: the verdant forests cut to make the logs, the logs shipped and milled to make the lumber, the lumber dried and trucked and stacked and finally, measured and cut and assembled into floors, walls, and rafters. Each and every step along the way to homeownership is at its heart a claim on our world's bounty of natural resources and on the labor necessary to extract them. One might argue that the lumber, at least, is renewable, but the same argument cannot be made on behalf of the fossil fuels utilized to harvest, transport, and process it. The same argument cannot be made for the asphalt roofing shingles, a petroleum by-product. Or for many of the other myriad products that in aggregate compose the modern American home.[18]

In other words, the house is a product of the natural world. It was called forth from dense forests, from deep oil fields, and from the sweat that beaded on the brows of numerous workers; these are the entities that truly "paid" for the structure with a percentage of their assets: the worker's time, the forest's lumber, the oil field's bounty of concentrated labor. Of course, to an extent we *all* pay for the house, because the resources utilized are part of humanity's underlying reserves, on which we depend for

---

[18] In fact, contemporary construction materials are increasingly made of nonrenewable resources. Vinyl siding has replaced cedar clapboards; vinyl flooring often stands in place of wood floors. Some builders even use plastic lumber.

the essentials of our very survival. Indeed, the only things of real value in the entire exchange are the resources that have been shaped into a house, which have been extracted from the true economy via nothing more than a promise to pay, symbolized by digital numbers in a computerized account ledger.

There is one other aspect of the money-as-debt model that exacerbates the harm passed along to the general populace: This promise to pay dilutes the money supply, which in turn causes a drop in the value of everyone's savings because when the supply of money increases faster than the inventory of available goods and services, prices tend to rise. On a loan-by-loan basis, the drop in value is slight, even imperceptible, but over time, loan by loan by loan, the losses add up, and we find ourselves hard pressed to maintain our standard of living, much less afford the very basics of human survival. This is what we commonly call "inflation," and we think of it as rising prices, although the true definition of the word relates to the supply of money. Rising prices are merely a symptom of a money supply that increases faster than the total quantity of goods and services. If I were an economist, I'd call rising prices a "lagging indicator" of inflation. Fortunately, I'm not.

It is interesting—and somewhat dispiriting—to consider what happens as the money supply is diluted in a way that exacerbates income inequality,[19] which is precisely what has happened over the past few years. In 2010, the top 1 percent of earners captured 93 percent of the gains in personal income. Given this disparity, is it any surprise that lower income earners have been forced to go deeper and deeper into debt? And given that the majority of new debt is simply loaned into existence, it effectively dilutes the money

---

[19] The exacerbation of income inequality based on inflating money supply is primarily due to the fact that most wealthy people invest in ways that increase their financial wealth faster than the rate of inflation. Meanwhile, those in the lower income tiers simply don't have the assets or the investing savvy to do anything but hang on by the skin of their teeth.

supply, which only accelerates the process of eroding both our purchasing power and our underlying true wealth.

As we examine the way in which money is created, what begins to take shape is an absurdist scenario, and it occurs to me that more than any other reason, this almost surreal absurdity explains why discussions of monetary policy and design are so rare in workaday America. The workings of our money system and the manner in which it pits us against the environment, each other, and ultimately ourselves is so nonsensical that it becomes repellant; we know that it simply cannot work, that we cannot continue to leverage claims on finite resources with an infinite means of making those claims. Perhaps we even know, somewhere deep in our consciousness, that the increasingly commodified and monetized nature of contemporary American society is driving wedges between us all. Yet we also know that we have become dependent on these commodified relationships and resources in which they trade, and so we are presented with a sobering dichotomy: Our contemporary money system cannot work. *It must work.* It cannot. *It must.* It's not hard to see why simply ignoring it becomes a compelling option.

But even for those who have never given a moment's thought to the underpinnings of our money and the strange truths that lurk within them, I wonder if there's some level of innate or instinctual understanding that there is something unseemly about the basic construct of money. "For the love of money is the root of all kinds of evil. Some people, eager for money, have wandered from the faith and pierced themselves with many griefs," Paul tells Timothy in scripture (Timothy 6:10). Has there always existed some degree of suspicion that the accumulation of money beyond our immediate needs is inherently bad?

Of course, money is only money, which is to say, it is merely a symbol and a representation of the resources underpinning all of humanity. It cannot be inherently evil or good; only we can imbue it with these values. But still I suspect that on some level, we understand how its accumulation, be it in actual cash or investments, erodes the sum total of true wealth.[20] In other words, to advantage ourselves in this regard is to disadvantage others. Perhaps we even understand that it erodes *us*, chipping away at our autonomy and relationships by depersonalizing the nature of exchange.

I often find myself wondering why people seek to accumulate large sums of monetary wealth. And then I inevitably wonder if I am crazy for even wondering this, given the depth and breadth of the acceptance that such accumulation is a worthy goal. I would be remiss to suggest that no one else questions this assumption—clearly, Erik does, as do many others—but there is little doubt that the vast majority of Americans have been raised inside cultural, social, and educational systems that promulgate the righteousness of monetary and physical asset accumulation. It has become part and parcel of the American Dream that we hold up for ourselves and the rest of humanity to admire and strive for. So even to question it sometimes feels uncomfortable. What am I, a *socialist*?

Perhaps I am, although I'm not terribly interested in how my musing aligns with any particular political ideology. Instead, I'd rather consider the conditions that have given rise to the assumption of accumulated wealth. What is it, specifically, that drives a culture to embrace the notion of individualized asset hoarding in excess of what could reasonably be considered necessary to meet immediate or even medium-term needs?

I'm going to take this opportunity to give credit where credit is due and insert a passage from Charles Eisenstein's book *Sacred Economics*, which has had a profound impact on how I view issues

---

[20] Not to get all biblical on you again, but this might explain why in Matthew 19:23 Jesus told his disciples, "I tell you the truth, it is hard for a rich man to enter the kingdom of heaven."

of money and wealth: "In the context of abundance, greed is silly; only in the context of scarcity is it rational. The wealthy perceive scarcity where there is none. They also worry more than anybody else about money. Could it be that money itself causes the perception of scarcity? Could it be that money, nearly synonymous with the security, ironically brings the opposite? The answer to both these questions is yes."

Eisenstein rightly points out that many of the goods, services, and natural resources once considered part of our collective wealth—often known as "the commons"—have been claimed by the monetary realm. The groundwater becomes polluted by industrial waste, but don't worry, because you can always buy bottled water. And don't worry, because the fish that are no longer safe to eat from the rivers can instead be purchased from an industrial–scale fish farm. Services that not long ago were provided on a neighbor-to-neighbor basis—childcare, for instance, or food production—have been extracted from our communities, to be monetized, consolidated, and depersonalized, before being offered back to us, complete with price tag. Consider the current hoopla over so-called social media, which is little more than the monetization of our relationships. True, it costs nothing to use Facebook or Google, but that's only because the information we willingly provide—often, unawares, unless we've read through reams of legalese—is utilized by corporate entities to hone marketing pitches. To sell us stuff. As we do in the face of the commodification of most products and services, we fool ourselves into believing the pitch: In this case, that social media connects us to others and enriches our social lives. But of course every minute we spend "connecting" via the available mediums, while they scan our "content" for opportunities to profit from the exchange, is a minute we're not connecting with people face-to-face, in the real world. It is as if, having scraped the bottom of the barrel of obviously marketable (and occasionally, necessary) goods and services, there's nothing left to sell us but *us*.

As you might expect, when essential resources are monetized, they are imbued with a sense a scarcity. Consider the common economic phrase "supply and demand," generally used to explain pricing fluctuations. We accept as a truism the notion that the scarcer an item, the more it should cost (or, conversely, the more abundant a product, the *less* it should cost). And so as prices increase and more of our nonmonetary wealth is transferred to the monetary realm, we hoard more fervently than ever, creating a vicious cycle that transforms perceived scarcity into real scarcity, which in turn drives the perception of scarcity and . . . you get the point. Of course, the truly tragic consequence of this cycle isn't the damage it does to the hoarders. Sure, we might feel sympathy for those who have so completely given themselves over to the realm of money, but let's be real: At least they have a roof over their heads and food in their bellies. Rather, the true tragic outcome of our scarcity story is our inability or even unwillingness to connect those in need with *what* they need. The difficult truth is that the world does not lack for resources; it is simply the misallocation of resources that creates the perception that there is not enough to go around.

All of this is not to suggest that resource depletion is not real, or that we needn't embrace conservation. Clearly, we have extracted a fair chunk of our underlying wealth base in exhausting a broad spectrum of natural resources. We've overfished our waters; it's estimated that global fishing fleets are 200 percent to 300 percent larger than our oceans can sustain. We've overdrilled our oil and gas fields; recall that the United States now imports nearly 70 percent of its oil, up from just 8.4 percent 6 decades ago. And we've overfarmed our soils; according to Cornell University's David Pimentel, modern mono-crop agricultural practices are causing our farmland to erode at a rate that's 10 times greater than the rate of natural topsoil reformation. And that's just in the United States; even more troubling are the statistics for China and

India, where soil depletion is occurring at a rate 30 to 40 times faster than natural replenishment.

What's truly striking is that all of this is happening in the context of GDP growth that's based, as it has been for more than 30 years, almost entirely on debt. Since 1980, and continuing unabated until the economic crash of 2008 when our nation's rate of debt accumulation went over a cliff, the United States has not seen a single 3-month period during which economic growth expressed in dollars occurred faster than the growth of new debt. Here's another way of putting it: For more than 3 decades, every single dollar of economic growth has been offset by *more* than another dollar of accumulated debt. As recently as the mid-1970s, it cost the United States less than half-a-buck to generate a full dollar of GDP growth; recently, that ratio has risen eightfold, to 4:1. To create a single dollar of GDP growth now requires tacking four dollars onto our debt tab.

Our economic growth is illusory and has been for a generation or more. Whatever affluence we thought we had gained is merely a lie, obscured by the accumulation of debt, which itself exploits our true, underlying resource wealth. It's a twofold tragedy that will, by necessity, come to light. These imbalances cannot be fixed by simply increasing our debt burden; we have gone too far over the edge to "grow" our way out of our current predicament. This is where, in a sense, the neoconservative deficit hawks have it right; where they have it wrong, of course, is how they would seek to rebalance the scales. Or, I should say it's wrong for the overwhelming majority of our nation's citizens; in the minds of those who would prefer to uphold the status quo, the methodology of making cuts primarily to those programs that support poor and working class citizenry is very right, indeed.

But of course, this is not the only way to rebalance our economy. As Charles Eisenstein points out, our modern societal and economic arrangements are ripe with the low-hanging fruit of enormous waste. Our resources are feeding a system of vast inefficiency. We invest 11 calories of energy into every single calorie of food we produce, with most of those calories being consumed by processing, packaging, and transport, and, along the path from field to fork, we discard an estimated 40 percent of the food we grow. Over approximately the same period that our per dollar debt-to-GDP ratio rose from 0.5:1 to 4:1, we have increased our per capita daily calorie production from 3,026 to 3,900; over this same time frame, the segment of the population receiving food stamps has risen from 2 percent to more than 14 percent. Concurrently, the average American home nearly doubled in size, from 1,400 square feet to 2,700 square feet, a fact that becomes somewhat less impressive considering the nearly 12 million foreclosures since the beginning of 2008. What good is a big house if you get kicked out of it? At least those forced to live in their cars will have plenty of parking options: By some estimates, the United States now boasts eight parking spaces for every car.

The pattern is clear: In aspect after aspect of our lives, we are faced with a mirage of wealth behind which lurks the true condition of our society. Ironically, it is the very maintenance of these mirages that causes most of our societal ills. Year after year, we feed our real wealth to the illusion; in ways both physical and spiritual, we let ourselves go hungry, for no other reason than to keep the story alive.

I have come a long way from the sugarhouse, and I return to it now only briefly, to make this final point. Because, finally, I have come to understand what it is about this spot that so captures my imagination and compels me to consider matters of wealth and money against a backdrop that would seem to suggest neither.

It is because, as antiquated and decayed as they are, these

sugarhouse remains are no mirage. The story told by the industry that occurred under the roof that once sheltered my favorite foundation stone was a story of conscious economics, rooted in toil and nature's regenerative gift of sap. It was not fueled by the false abundance generated by oil. The process involved in this early sugaring venture was extractive, to be sure, but in a manner that by necessity respected the natural resource, with the recognition that maple trees, if exploited through overtapping, will age prematurely and die. There was no way to externalize the toll of this small enterprise, which traded the sweet distillation of all the efforts put forth for the pockets of cash that would provide those essentials that could not be produced on a farm. It would have been understood that the value of the sugar bush could not be measured solely in monetary terms because to do so would begin to erode its vitality over the long haul. This was not altruism, or at least not wholly; it was simple recognition of the limitations inherent in the trees that—spring, after spring, after spring—gave forth a portion of their lifeblood.

It is only when the true costs of industry and wealth accumulation are hidden that the illusion of abundance begins to take shape. Often, it is simple distance that creates the opacity, but just as frequently, it is the lie that is told by this illusion. It says that we can lay down the "burden" of accountability and simple honest work. It whispers that life is better when this weight is lifted from our shoulders and we join the school of fish swimming in unison along the river of false abundance. But we forget that the factors making this arrangement the norm enjoy little historical precedent; we forget that the load does not simply disappear; it merely shifts, to be borne by the environment and the less fortunate. The illusory, self-generating nature of money is not the only reason for this shift, but it underpins all other factors, for it serves as their enabler.

Which is to say, until we fix our relationship to money, we will fix very little else.

[CHAPTER SEVEN]

IN WHICH I GO FOR THE GOLD.

TO UNDERSTAND how it was that I came to find myself in the dim confines of a second-story apartment in the small city of Manchester, New Hampshire, watching an unemployed middle-aged man legally create money, or at least, something that he claimed was money, and intended to distribute as such, it will help to have a little background.

And although that background by necessity reaches hundreds of years into the past, I will begin with the date September 13, 2011, which is the day Republican congressman Ron Paul took a respite from his bid to earn the GOP presidential nomination so that he might preside over a legislative hearing titled "Road Map to Sound Money." Paul is a longtime student of monetary policy and an advocate for a return to precious metals–based currency; indeed, he is the only national political figure to speak on these issues in public with any frequency or passion. He is also chairman of the Domestic Monetary Policy and Technology Subcommittee, and, with his withering criticism of the Federal Reserve, a longtime thorn in the side of Federal Reserve Chairman Ben Bernanke.

Congressman Paul has a tendency to speak in a tone of mild surprise, but when he talks about monetary policy, his ire toward the status quo seems to ratchet things up a notch or two, and his tone becomes one of reserved, professorial concern. He began the hearing this way:

> The monetary issue has been an issue that I have been fascinated with and interested in for a long time. I became much more aware of the significance of this issue back in August of 1971, with the breakdown of the Bretton Woods Agreement. At that time I was convinced—and remain convinced—that we have ushered in a special age that probably did not exist, ah, in the same fashion ever before. And we now have been living for 4 decades with a total fiat world currency, and it has created a lot of problems for us. We as a congress have lived way beyond our means because the people of this country wanted us to live beyond our means. And the monetary issue of course is very significant because it actually facilitates the spending. Without the type of system of money that we have today, there would have been a limitation on the massive expansion of size of government, spending, taxes, debt, and the crisis that we're facing right now. But few are even thinking about monetary policy as a significant contributor to our economic problems we have today.

The good congressman continued in this manner for another minute or two, making brief swipes at the Federal Reserve and paper money, before he lowered the boom:

> Many of us have been thinking about this for many, many years (but) things could move rapidly. Currency destructions—the end of currencies—sometimes move much quicker than everybody dreams that it could. So a major crisis could come. It could come next month or next year or in a few years. To me, there's no guarantee that we have 5 or 10 years to keep studying this.

To understand Ron Paul's preamble, we need to talk a bit more about the evolution of America's monetary system and the nature of money itself. As you will see, this is not an uncomplicated topic, nor is it one that lends itself to being encapsulated within the context of a single chapter; indeed, entire books have been written about money and the workings of the system that controls its creation and distribution, and even those who have dedicated their lives to studying the subject admit that full comprehension often eludes them.

But that's okay; our purpose here is simply to understand, in fairly broad strokes, how we have come to this place, how money's role in our society has changed, and why it is that Ron Paul feels a sense of urgency when speaking of contemporary monetary policy.

When we consider that money in one form or another has existed since at least 5000 BC, it's fascinating to realize that our current monetary-related crises, as sweeping and historic as they are, appear as but a mere speck along the arc of humanity's relationship to money. Rather than begin at the beginning, if only because the beginning exists at a point so far in the rearview mirror of monetary history that it has little bearing on the issues at hand, let us move forward along this arc, to a point marked by the latter years of the 18th century. Specifically, let's begin with the Secretary of the Treasury Alexander Hamilton's Coinage Act of 1792, also known as "An Act establishing a Mint and regulating the Coins of the United States." True to its title, the Coinage Act established the United States Mint and oversaw production and distribution of the national currency.

Quality control and general veracity were particularly important because, at the time, a dollar was expected to embody a rather exacting unit of measure. It was to be a coin minted of 24.1 grams of pure 371.25-grain silver. This was not some arbitrary number that had come to Hamilton in fugue state; a precedent had been set by the Spanish milled dollar, often referred to as "pieces of eight," so named because these coins were customarily divided into eighths to make smaller denominations called "bits." Before—and for some time after—United States independence in 1776, pieces of eight were the prevailing currency, and they were minted throughout the colonies at a measure of—you guessed it—24.1 grams of pure silver per dollar.

Now, it just so happens that only a few years before the enactment of the Coinage Act of 1792, a wee document known as the United States Constitution was adopted. This is important because although the Constitution does not directly put forth a standard for the nation's currency, it does at least mention money twice. The first is in relation to the slave tax, which of course has long since been abandoned. The second is in relation to the Seventh Amendment, which states: "In Suits at common law, where the value in controversy shall exceed twenty dollars, the right of a trial by jury shall be preserved, and no fact tried by a jury, shall be otherwise re-examined in any Court of the United States, than according to the rules of the common law."

You may be wondering why this matters, and to be honest, to many people it doesn't seem to matter very much at all. But to Ron Paul and other sound money advocates, it is the foundation for their contention that not only is the contemporary Federal Reserve Note doomed to worthlessness, it's downright unconstitutional, too. How so? Well, if the dollar mentioned in the Constitution was known to consist of 24.1 grams of pure silver, and only such dollars were considered valid throughout this foundling nation, then naturally the only dollar that could forevermore be considered in keeping with the Constitution was one that measured precisely 24.1 grams of 371.25-grain silver.

Now, let's take into account the fact that although the dollar was precisely defined in terms of a certain silver measurement, larger denominations were minted in gold, based on a silver-to-gold ratio of 15:1. In other words, 15 ounces of silver was the equivalent of a single ounce of gold, and this was convenient because carrying around a couple of pounds of silver in the pockets of your woolen knickers was absolute hell on the lower back. But a funny thing started happening: The value of the yellow metal began to rise, and gold coins were being melted down almost as fast as they could be minted, since their weighed value was greater than their face value.

Under these circumstances, it did not take long for the dollar to deviate from its Constitutional roots. The first deviation of note occurred with the Coinage Act of 1834, whereby the 15:1 silver-to-gold ratio was declared obsolete, and a new ratio, reflecting gold's increased value, was set at 16:1. In effect, this was the first orchestrated devaluation of the US dollar, because whereas previous dollars had been backed by 1.6 ounces of gold, the new ratio meant that all future dollars would be backed by only 1.5 ounces of gold. In other words, on a weighed-value basis, the new dollar was worth 6 percent *less* than its predecessor.

The next devaluation was quick to come. In 1853, the weights of all US silver coins, with the notable exception of the one dollar coin, were reduced (the dime, for instance, dropped from 2.67 to 2.49 grams of silver). The not-exactly-surprising reaction is that people began to shun the devalued silver medallions, and the US currency became, effectively, one that was both backed by and minted from gold.

This worked just dandy for a time. Eight years, to be exact.

Then came the Civil War, and the United States found itself in a spot of bother, financially speaking. The problem was simple: Conflict is not a cheap date. It demands a steady flow of cash to pay, feed, clothe, and arm soldiers. But with a gold-backed money supply, your available funds are limited to a fixed quantity of metal. Sure, you can mine more, but no matter how many shovels you stick into the ground, you're unlikely to uncover gold at a rate greater than a war's capacity to spend it. True, you could simply revalue gold, but then the last thing you need in the midst of an all-consuming war is a massive currency revaluation. You can see the rub, can't you?

Now, one of the few absolute truths of monetary policy is that governments tend to make major shifts at times of crisis, and a nation standing on the brink of bankruptcy while mired in civil war is generally considered to be in crisis. It was rapidly decided that what was needed was a bit of financial innovation. This is a term we have come to associate with the sort of barely concealed sleight of hand that accounts for much of our contemporary economic malaise, but the trickery relating to the 1861 issuance of the US Demand Note seems almost quaint in comparison, having to do with the decision made by our nation's founding fathers that the government should not be granted the right to issue banknotes. This, one would assume, ruled out federal printing and distribution of paper currency.

One would assume wrong, for while the US government didn't have the right to print currency, it had been granted the capacity to issue short-term debt, in the form of Treasury Notes. These had first been utilized during the War of 1812 and sporadically thereafter, as conditions warranted. One of these conditions was the great financial panic of 1837, which resulted from a rampant speculation in real estate and kicked off a deflationary depression that lasted for 5 years. The issuance of Treasury Notes was widely credited for, at least in part, pulling our nation out of the doldrums.

The financial malaise generated by the US Civil War was more grinding than acute, but it nonetheless provided the motivation to seek new ways to bolster the money supply. As such, it didn't take long before a loophole was recognized (the truly quaint part, I suppose, is that anyone thought a loophole necessary) and Demand Notes were issued under the framework of Treasury Notes. In essence, they *were* Treasury Notes, though they bore no interest and were issued in minor denominations of $5, $10, and $20. They also differed from previous notes in that the Treasury promised to pay "specie" (on demand) for the Demand Notes. In other words, one could redeem his or her Demand Notes for gold or silver coinage.

Unsurprisingly, the public's initial reaction—rooted in the suspicion that a piece of paper claiming to be the equivalent of a given allocation of gold or silver was not quite the same as the *actual* gold or silver—was tepid at best. A bird in the hand is worth two in the bush, and all that. Therefore, those who accepted the notes at all typically did so at a significant discount. This de facto devaluation forced Secretary of the Treasury Salmon P. Chase to embark on an energetic public relations campaign. He first agreed to accept his salary in Demand Notes and then, perhaps realizing that he'd effectively signed up for a considerable pay cut, issued a statement assuring the nation that the notes would be "at all times convertible into coin at the option of the holder" and that "they must always be equivalent to gold, and often and for many purposes more convenient and valuable."

Chase's words and actions propped up the notes for about 4 months before a shortage of gold and silver coinage forced banks to suspend specie payment. This had the predictable consequence of immediately eroding confidence in Demand Notes, a rather unsettling situation to which Congress responded by passing the Legal Tender Act of 1862. This laid the groundwork for the printing and distribution of the United States Note, a paper currency that carried the following promise: "This Note is Legal Tender for All Debts Public and Private Except Duties On Imports And Interest On The Public Debt; And Is Redeemable In Payment Of All Loans Made To The United States."

One might reasonably ask: *Why does all of this matter?* This is a question that could rightly be answered in numerous ways, at length. But the immediate answer I believe to be most crucial to understanding the current state of American monetary policy is that the United States Note, which was really just a modified version of the Demand Note, was America's first nationally distributed fiat currency.

As it relates to money and monetary policy, *fiat* refers to a currency that holds value only because a government says so. "Let it be done," said the leader, and it was done. That's the sort of value I'm talking about, although it should be noted that the United States Note was, for a time, backstopped by gold. Until 1933, you could actually redeem your dollars for gold at any bank, at the rate of $20.67 per ounce. In other words, although few people actually did commerce in precious metals, the paper dollar essentially served as a deposit slip for gold. It was still fiat in the sense that it depended on a collective faith that it would and should be granted value equivalent to gold, but that faith was supported by the knowledge that a physical asset actually existed.

This exchange mechanism was extinguished in 1933 by President Franklin Delano Roosevelt, with the signing of Executive Order 6102, which expressly prohibited private ownership of gold in excess of 5 ounces (remember, at the time the price of gold was fixed at $20.67 per ounce, so we're talking about $100 or so). This was yet another form of "financial innovation" at a time of economic malaise—in this case, the Great Depression—which Roosevelt sought to remedy by raising the price of gold to $35 per ounce. This had the effect of devaluing the dollar by nearly half, and it meant that the government's gold holdings were suddenly convertible to nearly twice as many dollars. The result? With a few strokes of his pen Roosevelt had generated a handsome $2.8 billion in "profit." Most of this sudden windfall was deposited into the newly created Exchange Stabilization Fund, intended to influence foreign exchange markets for the purpose of stabilizing the woozy dollar.

Clearly, there was never any serious intent of prosecuting American citizens for gold ownership and subjecting them to the maximum penalty of a $10,000 fine, 10 years in prison or, if someone was having a really bad day, both. In fact, over the 4 decades the law was in effect (it was repealed in 1974), only one person was indicted for refusing to surrender his gold; the charges were ultimately dropped, but the government's right to confiscate the gold was upheld.

Of course, it is no coincidence that 6102 was signed at the zenith of the Great Depression; the country was in dire straits and Roosevelt had his New Deal to finance. By ending the exchangeability of dollars for gold, Roosevelt had essentially removed all accountability from the currency distribution process and paved the way for unencumbered printing. Sure, the dollar was still pegged to gold at least in theory, but given that gold ownership in excess of 5 ounces was illegal, it was at best a symbolic connection.

Not surprisingly, there was a significant downside to Roosevelt's "innovation," which amounted to little more than a 41 percent devaluation of the dollar and an immediate increase in the US money supply. The implications were not confined to the United States, because the depreciated US currency was an impediment to other countries that wished to export goods to the preeminent consumer nation. So they did the only obvious thing: They devalued their currencies, too, while at the same time restricting much of their trade to nations that operated under a shared currency. To put it mildly, this was not particularly good for the global economy.

Then came the Bretton Woods agreement mentioned in Congressman Paul's preamble, and if you're looking for the precise moment that an interconnected, globalized, and heavily manipulated monetary system took wings, this is it. Bretton Woods is a resort town situated in the shadows of New Hampshire's 6,288-foot Mount Washington, which owns the dubious renown of being home to the world's worst weather. It's a region of breathtaking scenery, backdropped by jagged peaks that etch against the sky, like a row of teeth from the remains of some prehistoric beast that roamed the earth in a time before anyone even knew what money was. But perhaps most crucially, Bretton Woods represented the onset of the US dollar's rise to domination as the reserve currency of the world.

The agreement, which was hammered out by 730 delegates from all 44 Allied nations in July of 1944, established a framework for financial relations between the major industrial states of the mid-20th century. It was at Bretton Woods that the International Monetary Fund (IMF) was established, and it was at Bretton Woods that each participating country was obligated to peg its currency to the US dollar; fluctuations between currencies would be limited to 1 percent of their value. This was pitched as a stabilization effort, but of course it meant that in essence the United States controlled global monetary policy. Meanwhile, it was agreed that the dollar would again be backed by gold at the prevailing rate of $35 per ounce. In effect, the agreement created an international gold standard, with the US dollar serving as a bridge between individual currencies and the shiny yellow metal.

Was Bretton Woods good or bad? That depends very much on whom you ask and what time frame you consider. There's little question that the agreement generated a period of much-needed economic stability following the twin upheavals of the Great Depression and World War II (remember the golden rule:

Shifts in monetary policy are almost always concurrent with economic crises); with individual currencies marching in lockstep, the paralyzing fear of sudden and massive currency devaluations—rampant during the Depression—was eliminated. This paved the way for sustained growth in trade and the expansion of capitalist markets.

No country benefited from this more than the United States, which suddenly held the keys to the metaphoric global lockbox. As master of the global reserve currency, the United States essentially became banker to the world. This happened at a particularly convenient time, because many of the world's major economies were deeply in debt from war expenditures. To pay that debt, they pawned their gold reserves for dollars, which only the United States Treasury could print. As such, American bankers were able to accumulate tremendous stores of gold, which they exchanged for fiat currency that was deemed to be "good as gold," a promise that could only be kept so long as few countries actually called its bluff.

The inevitable bluff calling began in the mid-1960s, when foreign investors began to question the solvency of the United States, which was mired in the Vietnam War and spending like G.I. Joe on leave at Barbie's Dream House. The choice facing American political and economic leaders was stark: raise taxes or print dollars. They choose the latter. Not surprisingly, this course of action didn't sit very well with foreign nations that held significant dollar reserves and wished for the value of those reserves to remain undiluted by inflation. French president Charles de Gaulle was the first to come knocking, looking to exchange $300 million for the gold that supposedly backed it. Before long, other nations followed suit, and the United States, fearing the worst, took stock of its gold reserves. The resulting tally was sobering. The United States of America, holder of the world's reserve currency and caretaker of the shiny metal that supposedly backstopped the dollar's value, owned only 22 percent of the gold necessary to cover global dollar reserves.[21] Whoops.

All of which begins to explain the so-called Nixon Shock that swept through the global financial system like a summer thunderstorm in August of '71. Unilaterally, instantaneously, and without taking part in consultation with anyone beyond his closest advisors, President Nixon severed completely the dollar-to-gold exchange; this is what Ron Paul is talking about when he speaks of "the breakdown of the Bretton Woods Agreement." Suddenly, the United States dollar was backed by nothing more than the government's assurance that it would be accepted as legal tender wherever and whenever one wished to exchange it.

Whether or not this has been a good thing depends, again, on one's perspective. Certainly, eliminating the gold standard has provided monetary policy makers with a level of never-before-realized flexibility to manipulate a currency's value though printing, without fear that anyone might choose to redeem their money for gold. But, of course, this is a double-edged sword, particularly so in an era of interconnected financial markets through which nations trade debt as if they were school kids with an endless supply of baseball cards. Sure, a country can choose to inflate its money supply, but it does so at the risk of causing interest rates on its debt to rise. In other words, if China perceives that the United States is diluting its money supply via increased printing, it will demand increased return on its investments to make up for the erosion in value of these investments over time.

---

[21] What the United States feared, of course, was a "bank run" on its meager gold holdings. It's interesting to realize that in the context of modern banking, reserve holdings of 22 percent would be considered the pinnacle of responsibility. Indeed, this is why the banking industry is so fearful of bank runs: The money simply doesn't exist to pay out the account balances of more than a small percentage of depositors at any one time.

The belief that the United States should revert to a gold standard has widespread, if not exactly ubiquitous, support—although these days few dare utter the phrase "gold standard." Indeed, the movement's term of choice is now "sound money," a shift of vernacular that was itself a sound decision, given the marginalization of gold advocates in the latter half of the 20th century. One who reveres the metal has come to be known as a "gold bug," and the metal itself is often called a "barbarous relic," a nod to the monetary theorist John Maynard Keynes, who coined the term in 1924. Keynes was a pivotal figure in the Bretton Woods agreement and, according to rumor, the very reason the delegates met in New Hampshire, rather than the more logical locations of New York or Washington, DC: Keynes had a bad heart, and worried that his ticker couldn't take the stifling heat of the city in summer (he may have been right to trust his instincts; Keynes died of a heart attack 2 years later).

Leaving policy aside, there are certain pragmatic factors that make gold (and to a lesser extent, silver) an ideal token of exchange. For starters, it's relatively rare, a quality that imbues it with a degree of inherent desirability and all but assures that large quantities of human energy and natural resources will be expended in search of it. Second, it's virtually impervious to the elements: Beyond a bit of discoloration, neither gold nor silver is likely to degrade via exposure, and both metals are extremely durable. A gold coin is not going to wear out, no matter how much you fondle it. Third, both metals—gold in particular—are fairly malleable, making the minting of coins, as well as the formation of less formal weighed chunks and flakes a relatively simple affair.[22] And finally, as sound money advocates are keen to remind us, and as we

[22] For example, let's say you want to buy a loaf of rye bread, which your neighbor will happily sell you for a half-gram of gold. But shoot: All you have is a 2-gram nugget. What to do? Simply break out a pair of jeweler's scissors and a gram scale, and the deal will get done.

have seen, gold and silver have enjoyed a long-standing monetary precedence.

Attempts to return gold and silver to their monetary origins have come and gone in recent decades, but none have come so close to achieving widespread circulation—and therefore, viability—as the Liberty Dollar. The Liberty Dollar was the brainchild of a voluble man named Bernard von NotHaus, co-founder of the Royal Hawaiian Mint Company and self-proclaimed "monetary architect."

The Liberty Dollar was released on October 1, 1998, in the form of gold and silver coins and paper bills, the latter of which was described by von NotHaus as "warehouse receipts." The idea was markedly similar to the original gold standard backing United States Notes: Every bill represented an actual portion of gold or silver, held for the bearer in Coeur d'Alene, Idaho, at Sunshine Minting, which produced the Liberty Dollar coinage as well as blank coins for the US Mint. One could, both in theory and in practice, redeem Liberty Dollar bills for actual gold or silver.

It was an auspicious time to launch a sound money currency; on the day the Liberty Dollar was released, the national debt stood at $5,540,570,493,226.32 (let's dispense with all those bothersome commas and just call it $5.5 trillion, shall we?), reflecting a steady rise from about $2 billion at the turn of the century. In other words, over the preceding 98 years, the national debt had grown at a rate of about $56 billion annually. Alarming, perhaps, if one paused to think about it, but slow enough that few did. But over the next decade, the rate of growth would pick up just a bit, to approximately $500 billion a year; the current rate of growth is over $1 trillion annually. Both the rapidly escalating pace and alarming total of America's debt was becoming harder to ignore.

Ron Helwig was one of those paying attention. Helwig's interest in monetary policy was fomented just as the Liberty Dollar was gaining steam, when he was presented with a $5 silver Liberty medallion as a door prize for being the first person to show up at meeting for an objectivist group.[23] That small medallion of silver had a lasting impact on Helwig. "I moved to New Hampshire in 2005, and by 2007 I felt settled enough to say, 'Okay, it's time to get serious about the Liberty Dollar,'" he told me. Helwig had moved to the Granite State as part of a political migration known as the Free State Project, which seeks to populate New Hampshire with 20,000 freedom-loving libertarians.[24] When I stopped in at Helwig's nondescript apartment in January 2012, the organization was closing in on 1,000 members, only 19,000 short of its goal. At number 103, Helwig had been among the migration's first wave, and this fact seemed to please him.

Helwig saw the Liberty Dollar as an opportunity to rally around a sound currency, and also thought it might free him from the rut of what he calls "debateatariansim," a term he coined to describe the libertarian tendency to spend more time debating, and less time doing. So he arranged a meeting for fellow Liberty Dollar supporters, to discuss how they might best promote the currency.

To put it mildly, his timing stunk. Two days before Helwig's scheduled meeting, the FBI and Secret Service raided Liberty Dollar offices. At the time, there was somewhere in the range of

---

[23] Objectivism is a philosophy created by Ayn Rand; it is largely based on the belief that pursuit of one's own happiness is the highest calling, and that the only social system that can allow for the full expression of individual happiness is one that embraces individual rights via laissez-faire capitalism.

[24] Sound money policy is often linked to libertarian politics; this has been most famously expressed via the presidential campaign of Ron Paul, who has repeatedly called for the abolition of the Federal Reserve and a return to a metal-based currency. Depending on one's political viewpoint, the connection between sound money and libertarianism could be seen as either a blessing or a curse. In either case, it's worth pointing out that the two are not mutually exclusive, though they do seem to enjoy each other's company in a pizza-and-beer sort of way.

$75 million worth of Liberty Dollars in circulation. The agents seized gold, silver, and platinum, as well as nearly 2 tons of "Ron Paul Dollars." They took computers and files, and froze all Liberty Dollar bank accounts. Von NotHaus's Web site was taken down, and he was ultimately charged with counterfeiting and fraud. The US attorney handling the case called the minting and distribution of the Liberty Dollar "a unique form of domestic terrorism." The US attorney said: "While these forms of anti-government activities do not involve violence, they are every bit as insidious and represent a clear and present danger to the economic stability of this country." As of this writing, von NotHaus was awaiting sentencing, which could eventually include enough years to see him through the remainder of his natural life (he's nearly 70).

Despite the abrupt shift in the Liberty Dollar's fortunes, Helwig's meeting went ahead as planned. "It was sort of like 'Okay, what do we do now?' The consensus was that we want to be minting our own rounds." But what about the raid and subsequent arrest of von NotHaus? Hadn't that given pause to the notion of creating a currency? Not so, Helwig assured me, for he had recognized a key flaw in the Liberty Dollar model—the centralization of its operations and precious metal reserves. "I recognized the need to decentralize. It's like dealing drugs; you spread everything out so they can never fully stop you."[25]

To answer his question of what to do now, Helwig launched a currency he calls "Shire Silver," which consists of gold or silver strips he cuts from jeweler's stock. Each length of metal corresponds to a specific weight, as displayed by a small, electronic scale boasting one-hundredth-of-a-gram accuracy. Once he has achieved the proper weight (Helwig finds it helpful to use a precut length of drinking

---

[25] To be clear, Ron Helwig does not actually deal drugs; at least, not to my knowledge. He's merely analogizing the decentralization of money creation to the decentralization of the drug trade.

straw as a guide, although the weights he's dealing with are so minute—as little as one-twentieth of a gram—that even a slight bend in the wire can throw off his accuracy), Helwig sandwiches the gossamer strip of metal between two credit-card-sized pieces of plastic and runs the sandwich through a lamination machine.

I sat with Helwig for a couple of hours as he talked about and made money, his hands moving between coils of silver and gold, a pair of scissors, a digital scale, and the laminator. Outside, the sun shone brightly, but the window blinds were drawn, and Helwig possesses the milky pallor of one who spends the majority of his waking hours indoors. His thinning hair was cut short and emerged from his scalp in the spiked manner of a porcupine. He is heavyset and currently unemployed; he is a single father to a 20-month-old son, and he hopes soon to be making a livable income from Shire Silver. If it struck Helwig as ironic or simply dispiriting that he was depending on the success of his sound money currency to create an income denominated in Federal Reserve Notes, he didn't mention it.

To understand Helwig's sound money quest, and von NotHaus's before him, it's crucial to understand that the right to issue private currency is protected by the US Constitution, so long as one does not claim it to be "legal tender" and so long as one abides by the Constitution's directive: "Whoever, except as authorized by law, makes or utters or passes, or attempts to utter or pass, any coins of gold or silver or other metal, or alloys of metals, intended for use as current money, whether in the resemblance of coins of the United States or of foreign countries, or of original design, shall be fined under this title or imprisoned not more than five years, or both." In other words, if you're going to issue a private currency, you'd better be damn sure it's not mistaken for Federal Reserve Notes, or you're likely to wind up in the hoosegow. Still, an estimated 8,000 currencies have been issued in our nation's history, although most of these failed to gain much traction.

Helwig endured 2 years of trial and error determining how best to mint his own coinage. A log splitter was employed because of the tremendous hydraulic pressure it was capable of exerting, but the process was found to be "very slow and cumbersome." Ditto a hydraulic car jack. And the dies used to mold the metal into shape were themselves a problem: A die set might last for only 100,000 pressings and would cost upwards of $2,000. This was simply too much overhead for a fledgling currency to absorb. Besides, the upfront cost would impede efforts to decentralize production per Helwig's drug-dealing analogy, and this violated a key tenet.

Eventually, Helwig settled on the laminate idea, which met all of his requirements for the minting of a metals-backed currency. The lamination equipment was fairly portable and, because it was cheap (minus the computer, the whole setup cost less than $500), it encouraged replication. Best yet, he could "print" small quantities of minor denominations quickly and cost effectively.

Helwig's decision to tinker in the monetary realm is rooted in his having mildly antisocial tendencies. Fairly early on along his libertarian path, he identified two national systems he felt needed reform: money and education. But the latter, he realized, would necessitate human interaction on a scale he found somewhat discomfiting. "Education system fixes require you to be going out and talking to people," he told me. "I'm not really a social person." I glanced toward the window and the feeble light attempting to infiltrate the room. "My dream in college was to get a job working on a computer in a back corner where no one would bother me."

At the time of my visit, approximately 18 months had passed since the launch of Shire Silver, which had occurred at the 2010 PorcFest, an annual Free State Project gathering that, to the largest extent possible, exists outside the purview of the federal government. Trade in metals is encouraged, and moonshine and marijuana are widely available. In those 18 months, Helwig had distributed more than $30,000 worth of Shire Silver, not including the two cards he gave me in exchange for $5. One card contained a half-gram of silver; the other, one-twentieth of a gram of gold.

For a moment, I studied the pair of cards, which had just come out of the laminator and were still warm. Maybe it was merely the effect of the plastic, but both metals looked disappointingly dull and laughably inconsequential; the length of gold was no more substantial than a strand of hair. This was unsettling enough, but furthermore, I realized I had no way to validate its authenticity. I mean, I trusted Helwig; I did not for a second believe he was trying to rip me off. But what if *he* had been ripped off? And then I wondered: What if I couldn't find anyone to accept the cards as payment? What if they just sat in my wallet, looking for an opportunity to be spent? Could they really be counted as money? Because no matter how "real" or "sound" Helwig's currency was, if it couldn't be spent, it held little value to me. Thank goodness I hadn't sprung for the half-gram gold card, which would have cost me a full 40 bucks.

It wasn't long before I stumbled on the ultimate irony. Sound money advocates tend to wax poetic about the ability of precious metals to act as a "store of value" and about how a metals-backed currency would stem the erosion of the US dollar. They point to charts that show the dollar losing more than 90 percent of its value over the past 100 years, while the value of gold and silver has remained steady and, in recent years, spiked. But of course, the value they speak of is measured in dollars, and metals merchants are only too happy to exchange their product for Federal Reserve Notes at the prevailing rate, as Helwig had just demonstrated.

And so a strange thought occurred to me, one which I did not share with Helwig, if only because it is so heretical to the belief system of sound money advocates, that I feared his reaction: *What if it is exactly the opposite?* What if it is actually the US dollar, with all its fiat-based, inflationary temptation, that gives value to the metals? Because without this means of exchange, the metals and metal-based currencies like Shire Silver exist in something of a vacuum. I'd traded a small handful of Federal Reserve Notes for the nearly microscopic holding of gold and silver I now tucked into my wallet, but until I could find someone to take them off my hands, either for a good or service, or in exchange for *their* currency, they were worthless to me. There was no more intrinsic value to the metals than there was to the $46 in cash I'd carried with me to Manchester, New Hampshire. I reflected for a minute on my newly acquired Shire Silver dollars. I couldn't eat them, I couldn't wear them, and I couldn't burn them for warmth. I could only hope that someone else would recognize their value, and exchange them for the essentials of human survival.

I left Helwig's somewhat dispirited. I'd hoped he be able to show me how sound money might return prudence and stability to monetary policy, and therefore begin to shift our relationship to money in a way that would mitigate some of its dysfunction. Instead, what I'd seen felt like a mirror of the money system I already knew, and to an extent, Helwig didn't dispute this. "There's no such thing as 'intrinsic value,'" he told me, when I pointed out that no matter how much gold or silver I held, it did me little good if no one would accept it as currency. "Intrinsic value is simply based on people's historical relationship to an item." In other words, like the dollar, gold and silver have value only because we agree they do. In a sense, they are themselves fiat, not by the law of government, but by the people's decree.

About 2 miles up the road from Helwig's apartment, I stopped to fill my Subaru with gas. To be sure, I was distracted, thinking as I was about gold and silver and money and intrinsic value, so perhaps it's no surprise that when I reached into my wallet for my credit card, my fingers found the half-gram of Shire Silver, instead.

Twice I jabbed it into the slot on the pump's face, wondering why the stupid machine would not accept my Visa card, my nominal money, my feeble promise to pay.

But of course it wasn't my Visa. It was a half-gram of real silver, imprisoned in a plastic cage the exact size, shape, and weight of a credit card. For a heartbeat and if only for the sake of the story that might result, I considered seeking out the manager, to see if I might convince him to accept my silver as partial payment. But it was late, and I was pretty sure I knew what the answer would be. So I tucked my sound money back into my wallet and whipped out the standard plastic with its raised numbers and magnetic strip. A minute later, having paid nothing but the promise of a payment, I was back on the road.

Is it presumptuous for me to declare that precious metals are not money? Or, at the very least, not *sound* money? Perhaps it is presumptuous, and I cannot deny the depth of their historical precedence as money. But to me, the gold-as-money ideology is riddled with flaws, some of which it shares with fiat currency, some of which it owns in whole.

The first, and to me most important, of these flaws is that the extraction of such metals is dependent on mining practices and an industrial supply chain that degrades the environment to an extent that is rarely rivaled in the modern world. And that's sure as heck saying something. It's estimated that about 20 percent of gold is mined illegally, and this gold, called "wildcat" gold, is extracted with the use of mercury, which readily binds to the metal and eliminates the onerous, time-honored practice of manual panning, which is fantastically boring (I know; I've done it). But this isn't even the worst of it, because once the gold has been amalgamated, the mercury is burned off, at which point it becomes an airborne gas, capable of dispersing across thousands of miles. The average annual mercury release attributed to gold extraction is 1,400 tons; with the exception of coal burning, no other industry releases as much mercury into the environment. And this is just wildcat mining; the ramifications of legalized mining practices (which do not include mercury, but are somewhat less than benign) aren't exactly pretty. In one Peruvian town, where a smelter produces gold bullion bars, 99 percent of the children suffer from severe lead poisoning due to the off-gassed lead by-product of the smelting process. And in 1996, Pik Botha, the South African minister for mineral and energy affairs at the time, estimated that each ton of gold mined cost one life and a dozen serious injuries. In 2010, there were 2,652 tons of gold mined globally; I'll leave the depressing math to you. If gold were returned to its "rightful" place in our monetary system, demand would surely rise, and with it, the tremendous toll of human life and suffering. Each of Helwig's strands of gold and silver, no matter how gossamer, carry the little acknowledged weight of human sacrifice.

To my mind, the deleterious environmental and humanitarian consequences inherent in gold mining are enough to disqualify it as an acceptable mechanism of exchange. To rely on a medium that so profoundly violates the very foundation of our health and well-being is nothing short of insanity, although it is a familiar type of insanity. Unsurprisingly, such insanity is conveniently overlooked by those advocating for gold's return to monetary status and those who hold the metal as an investment, and I believe this oversight can be explained by two simple truths. One is that most gold mining (and therefore, the visible devastation) is conducted in faraway places; China, Australia, and South Africa are the leading gold-producing nations. The other is that money is a steadfast master, and we forgive ourselves much in our pursuit of it.

Precious metals fail from a strictly pragmatic standpoint, too. Like physical fiat currency, gold and silver are concentrated stores of value that are subject to confiscation, be it one imposed by government or by thievery. Neither is unprecedented, although those whose imaginations run toward an outright collapse of our printed currency, rather than a peaceful transition to something more durable, rarely acknowledge it. To them, metals are the only true safe haven, and no one should be without an Armageddon stash in preparation for the inevitable decline of the Federal Reserve Note.

That our currency will wither and eventually die, I have little doubt; every fiat currency in the history of humankind has done so, and there's no reason to think the Federal Reserve Note is any different. That such a collapse could happen catastrophically seems at least plausible. But I have serious doubts in either case that a cache of gold will prove a viable antidote. In a scenario such as this, with the US dollar approaching the value inherent in the paper on which it is printed, is it really plausible that there will not be prying eyes, ears, and hands, all alert to the presence of the shiny stuff? It is possible—even likely—that physical metals (as opposed to metal stocks or exchange-traded funds) will retain and even gain value in such an environment, but what good is that if the metals cannot be used for fear of confiscation or theft? Gold is easy to hide, particularly if you have access to a patch of dirt and a shovel, but the notion that hidden gold is viable currency has an "if a tree falls in the forest, does it make a sound?" ring to it. In short, what good is money if you can't use it?

Still, we needn't entertain such extremes to uncover a fundamental flaw in the assumption that a metals-backed currency is somehow more "sound" or "real" than fiat. The argument that metals have intrinsic value (an argument that even Ron Helwig discounts) is easily disproven. Sure, it is true that both gold and silver hold certain value to industry, but even that value is framed by a complex web of arrangements that suggest what it should be relative to all other goods and services. In other words, nothing has value in a vacuum; everything is relative.

Admittedly, I find it unsettling to consider the inherent worthlessness of the Federal Reserve Notes in which I am paid and which I rely upon to support my family. Even a year's worth of them—a full 35,000 dollar bills, give or take a few—is barely enough to do more than roast a woodchuck or two, should end times neuter their symbolic value. It is comforting to think they might be redeemable for *something*, though I'm at a loss to explain precisely why this idea comforts me, or why that something should be a product that wreaks such incredible havoc. Sure, gold is real, but then, so is a dog turd. If "real" is all we're looking for, why not choose something that is at the very least benign? Why not choose something that might serve some purpose other than sitting like a lump and shining in the sun?

All of this was leading me down a path to a question I've thus far managed to skirt: *What is money?* Furthermore, does its physical form have any actual bearing on its value and our relationship to it? Sound money advocates claim it does; they believe that if our currency were backed by precious metals, we would be unable to readily dilute our monetary supply. But as we have seen, the history of metals-backed money is riddled with devaluations and "innovations"; there's no quality inherent in gold or silver that makes it immune to such machinations.

Of course, money has been different things to different peoples, at different times. Cowry shells, barley, beads, whale teeth, cows,[26] even immobile rocks: On Yap, an island in the western Pacific Ocean, the currency is Rai, which consists of doughnut-shaped disks of calcite, as big as 12 *feet* across.[27] In other words, money doesn't have to be green; it doesn't have to be easily divisible. Nor must it provide milk or meat; hell, it doesn't even have to

[26] The term "pecuniary," which means "related to money," is derived from the Latin *percuniarius*, which is defined as "wealth in cattle."

[27] Islanders have adopted the US dollar for everyday transactions, but Rai is still utilized for ceremonial exchange.

be portable. The truth is, money can be *anything*. Its only requirement is that it be recognized as such.

The point I'm trying to make is that the concept of money as embodying a distinct physical form is a myth. Money is not a thing; indeed, it might not even be a noun. It seems to me that money is actually an aggregation of the cultural, financial, and social arrangements created around the exchange of goods and services. As such, it matters not what it looks, feels, or smells like (or, in the case of cows, tastes like). It needn't embody any particular attribute, other than our collective faith in its veracity as a medium of exchange. But even this faith needn't be national or even global; successful regional currencies like Ithaca Hours, in Ithaca, New York, or BNotes, in Baltimore, Maryland, demonstrate that there can and perhaps should be limits to money's geographical scope.

As seductive as it might be to blame our multitudinous woes—inequality, environmental degradation, excessive national debt, and so forth—on the physical characteristics of our monetary system, to do so would be to ignore the core truth that money is so much more than a thing. What is "real" and "sound" about money cannot be found in a symbolic totem; it can only be found in our actions and intent. Changing our monetary system for the better will require more than merely swapping one symbol for another; it will require nothing less than the resetting of our associations, expectations, and habits, on both societal and individual levels.

In one sense, this is immensely more difficult because it demands that we change more than a simple medium of exchange. In another sense, it is immensely easier, for there is no need to reimagine and revalue our currency, nor live through the chaos that would inevitably result.

It's simple, really: We need only reimagine and revalue ourselves.

[CHAPTER EIGHT]

IN WHICH I GRAPPLE WITH THE DIFFERENCE BETWEEN "VALUE" AND "WORTH" AND LEARN ABOUT THE CURRENCY OF TRUST.

I DID NOT see much of Erik over the summer. Partly, this was because he wasn't around very much; he'd embarked on a trip to Montana, traveling with an environmental activists' group to an annual gathering. They'd taken to the road in a small bus, and I amused myself by imaging the shaggy group of them rolling down America's highways on their quest for eco-justice. Every so often, a postcard would arrive, bearing Erik's handwriting, which was surprisingly precise and recounted his experiences in graceful, almost poetic detail: "Uncle Bob who lives out here took me to Eagle Creek (where there was indeed an eagle, probably the tenth I've seen out here!) where we hiked in 6.5 miles, sometimes holding on to metal cables as we scaled cliff walls, to a 100+ foot waterfall! With a tunnel fifty feet up that walked through behind the raging water! It was crazy and beautiful on epic perportions [sic]. Big bright rainbows rose off the mist of the pool below." And: "It's hot here where the valleys are wide and the mountains so high, snow covered peaks and magical spots like the wild undeveloped hot springs where I went and took a nice long soak with some friends this mornin' at dawn. The spring was surrounded by giant old cedar at least four feet wide! Before the bath I was awoken in the twilight by haunting howls of western kinds of coyotes."

With Erik out of town gazing at eagles and rainbows and soaking his bones in wilderness hot springs like some bohemian spa master, I passed much of my free time wandering the woods, considering both his and my relationship to money and wealth. The more I walked, the more aware I became of how my perceptions had shifted since I'd met Erik. At first, I'd regarded him primarily as someone who did without, and, as such, I'd unconsciously ascribed to him a monkish quality. In my mind, he was an ascetic, an abstainer, a man driven by principle to live in this particular way. To be sure, I was cognizant of the benefit of his chosen path, and at times, as previously noted, deeply envious. It wasn't so much that I envied his life's pragmatic qualities or quotidian moments but rather the emotional and perhaps spiritual benefits that enabled him to survive and even thrive in the absence of monetary abundance. Of course, I was also struck by the exceptional freedom he had forged for himself, and, equally, I was impressed by—and hoped to find within myself—the equanimity that he seemed to embody day in, day out.

There were two problems intrinsic to this line of thinking, and the more time I spent with Erik, the more glaring they became. The first was that, to be candid, I wasn't sure I *wanted* to do without. Rather, what I desired was the serene contentment that emanated from Erik; he was like a fire on a cold day, radiating warmth and comfort, and I basked in it. This felt good and right, but it was not enough to warm myself at his side. In short, I wanted to be a producer of serene contentment, not merely its consumer.

Fair enough, I suppose. After all, who *wouldn't* want to be a source of such a thing? Who *wouldn't* want to be able to find great happiness and gratitude against a backdrop of such simple means? Even in our consumption-addled culture, such qualities are imbued with honor and nobility: We admire those who embody them, even as we quietly acknowledge our own inability to adopt these tenets for ourselves. And in this regard, it pains me to say, I am no different. To be sure, I'd made sound choices regarding money and affluence long before I met Erik, and these choices had done much to spring me from the debt trap and bestow upon me a certain degree of the very freedom I so envied. And to be sure, my family and I had long before set our expectations for our standard of living somewhat lower than is generally assumed in contemporary America. But these standards had been in large part set by the fiscal realities of my chosen occupation. In other words, they didn't arise through some conscious act of my own, but rather were the default response to my modest income and debt-related phobia.

I worried that achieving Erik's serene contentment and equanimity would by necessity demand a voluntary reduction in my family's standard of living, from a level that hovered at heights Erik had never realized in his adult life. There is a widely accepted phenomenon in behavioral science circles known as "myopic loss aversion." In short, myopic loss aversion describes humans' innate tendency to be more affected by losses than gains. In other words, the pain of a loss is more affecting and impactful than the pleasure of a gain. The phenomena is most often associated with investing and gambling, which of course have more in common than not. Studies of both gamblers and investors have repeatedly shown that people tend to cash in on winning positions for relatively little gain,[28] while holding losing positions until they've been nearly wiped out. Both behaviors are explicit examples of an innate aversion to loss; the gain is capped for fear that it will turn sour, and the loss is extended because it's simply too emotionally devastating to close the position and take the hit.[29]

Of course, the notion that Erik might invest in the markets or be found hunched over a blackjack table in the presence of gambling chips, a Scotch on the rocks, and the sour smell of desperation was beyond absurd. And I wasn't too keen on these things myself. But then, gains and losses frequently occur beyond the monetary realm; myopic loss aversion might be most frequently associated with money or other assets, but it requires neither. As such, both Erik and I were as susceptible as the next fellow, although it occurred to me that perhaps Erik was somewhat advantaged in this regard, if only because he'd never achieved a particularly high standard of living. Here was a man whose definition of upward mobility could be found inside the confines of a 96-square-foot cabin, precariously perched on borrowed land. It struck me that it would be pretty damn hard to experience myopic loss aversion if you had nothing to lose, and I felt strangely jealous of the fact that having lived so much of his life without many of the assumed comforts and conveniences of contemporary American life, Erik could never know the pain of losing these things. Was my thinking convoluted? Perhaps. Probably. But if so, my skewed perspective only underscores the power of myopic loss aversion: Here I was, so afraid of facing a declining standard of living that I

---

[28] Of course, the dynamics of gambling, whereby wins often result in massive, against-all-odds windfalls, mean that gamblers sometimes don't have a choice to cash in early.

[29] This dynamic is quite visibly at play in the current practice of "extend and pretend" at many of our nation's largest financial institutions. Rather than marking assets to true market value, these institutions have been allowed to value them as if the financial and real estate crashes never happened, in hopes that a recovery will eventually restore them to precrash valuations.

was jealous of a man who would never know this fear, if only because he had never derived pleasure from that which a higher standard of living would supposedly have bestowed on him.

These presumptions may all be a bit unfair because of course Erik had plenty to lose. Furthermore, he'd recently leapfrogged to exponentially more commodious digs with the move to Heidi's place. It did not seem inconceivable to me that the relative opulence of his new digs (Toilet! Telephone! Internet access! Stairs, even!) might soften him over time, and that any potential slide downward to a lower standard of living—should events necessitate such a slide—could affect him in ways that observers of myopic loss aversion would recognize all too well.

But what did all this mean for myself? Was my fear of scaling back merely a textbook case of myopic loss aversion? And of course, my family complicated things. I could not make cuts in isolation; unlike Erik, who had only his own expectations to set and satisfy, my expectations and living standards were entwined with those of my wife and children. In the case of the former this was not a problem, for as I've previously noted, Penny was not merely an ally in the quest for cutbacks, but an instigator. Her desire to pick every last scrap of flesh off the bone of our family budget and general consumptive habits was nothing short of insatiable. I half expect to come home one day to find her ripping out the plumbing—in part because the scrap copper market is hot, and in part because indoor plumbing represents to her an untenable degree of luxury. Of course I exaggerate, but not much.

Mind you, I'm not complaining about Penny's mindset, in part because it relieves the pressure on me to direct my path in accordance with occupational or income-based factors. But the truth is, it places me in the somewhat discomfiting position of lacking a viable excuse for not acting on my desire to achieve at least a portion of Erik's Zen-like contentment, which I assumed was in part due to his studied avoidance of the moneyed economy. I simply couldn't pawn off my inaction on a spouse, because she was raring to join my friend in his quest.

Of course, there were the children to think about; at 7 and 10, the boys were coming of an age whereby they were likely to notice changes in our standard of living. Might they experience myopic loss aversion if things suddenly took a turn to the south? Might this not be a more traumatic experience for them than it would be for me, a grown man with the presumed advantage of emotional maturity? I did not even broach the subject with Penny, knowing full well how stridently she'd argue that the trauma of a declining standard of living, as defined by material goods and the comfort they provided, would be more than offset by our family's increased awareness of the natural world and the interconnectedness that was certain to evolve from embracing a more holistic abundance.

I disagreed with none of this. Yet I found it daunting to consider deeper cuts in my family's budget, which had already been pared to what I perceived to be a noble minimum. But was it, really? Because while Erik was subsisting on somewhere around $500 each month, most months we spent five or six times that.[30] Sure, there were four times as many of us, but two of them were children, with child-sized appetites. Furthermore, owing to their relatively isolated rural upbringing and our reliance on thrift stores, they possess little awareness of the manufactured toys and electronic gadgetry generally assumed to come with the territory of childhood in contemporary America. In other words, our boys are particularly cheap keepers, whose expectations for material abundance have been set lower than most of their contemporaries. Despite this, and despite my wife's (and to a lesser extent, my own)

---

[30] If you're quick with math, you can see that we spend pretty much everything we make. We do have some savings, but most of what might have gone into savings has instead gone toward the retirement of our debt.

concerted efforts, we'd created a life that demanded significant flows of cash; that there were opportunities aplenty to eliminate spending, I had little doubt. But did I want to? Not much, I had to admit.

And there was another profound misunderstanding in my understanding of Erik's relationship to frugality, one that had been slowly percolating its way toward the foremost of my consciousness: *Erik didn't think of himself as frugal.* Granted, this has been fairly obvious from the outset, if for no other reason than that he had told me so. And, in my defense, I'd picked up on it early on: *In one sense, he is the poorest person I know. It may already be obvious that in another sense, he is the wealthiest,* I wrote in the first chapter of this book. It wasn't a gratuitous observation; I believed it wholeheartedly, though I could not at that point provide an accounting of his wealth. But by now I'd spent the better part of a year examining Erik's unique version of prosperity, and I was beginning to feel more comfortable putting words to it.

In short, what I'd observed in Erik's life was an incredibly interconnected, interdependent community network that shared freely of its resources be they intellectual, physical, or material. The most obvious example was his cabin, built on a friend's land, largely by the labor of friends, with tools borrowed from friends. Erik had in large part usurped the moneyed economy by creating an economy of reciprocation, and he'd done so by building relationships within his community, using the human tools of trust, graciousness, compassion, and responsibility. "I know I could go to the hardware store and buy or rent the tools I need," he told me once, when I asked about the proliferation of borrowed implements at his half-finished cabin, which, I'm keen to point out, for a time included our compound miter saw, a $600 contraption that could cut through a two-by-six approximately 1,001 times faster than Erik's handsaw. "But I don't have to because there's an innate trust that I will return my friends' tools in good condition." He paused a moment. "I might even throw in a pound of beef or something in appreciation."[31]

Maybe it was simply because he was talking about hardware stores, but I remembered a passage I'd read recently in Lewis Hyde's book *The Gift: Creativity and the Artist in the Modern World*, which explores both gifts and monetary exchange. It is a fascinating book and should be considered essential reading for anyone interested in how money and the commodification of essential (and nonessential) goods and services have eroded our relationships to fellow humans and to nature. Here is the passage: "It is the cardinal difference between gift exchange and commodity exchange that a gift establishes a feeling-bond between two people, while the sale of a commodity leaves no necessary connection. I go into a hardware store, pay the man for a hacksaw blade and walk out. I may never see him again. The disconnectedness is, in fact, a virtue of the commodity mode. *We don't want to be bothered.*[32] If the clerk always wants to chat about the family, I'll shop elsewhere. I just want a hacksaw blade."

There are a couple of things I find fascinating about this passage. The first is that Hyde is comparing gift exchange to commodity exchange and then, in a later passage, actually defining that difference. A commodity, he explains, is that which is valued via a comparison to another item. This value allows the product to enter into the market, to be traded and ultimately consumed by whoever can scrape together enough dough to pay for it. Take oil, for instance, which is pretty much the ultimate commodity. Everybody needs it, and because one barrel of oil is essentially indistinguishable from another, they can be traded across great distances, without careful inspection.

In a sense, oil only has value once it has entered a market in which that value can be defined by a metric that is universally (or

---

[31] We got our saw back in perfect condition. Still waiting on the beef, though.

[32] Emphasis mine.

nearly universally) acknowledged, accepted, and understood. It is not that oil is not worth anything without a price tag attached to it; obviously, it still embodies the same incredible density of energy and expression of human labor whether or not it is actually priced. But it is the *price* that allows it to be assigned a standardized *value*, and it is the value that allows it to be brought under the umbrella of the commodity market.

A gift, says Hyde, is very different: It does not have value; it has *worth*. A gift is not homogenous, and its worth is based on innumerable factors, many of which are too personal to ever translate into value. Therefore, a gift cannot be assigned a price, or at least, it cannot be priced to a standard that is universally understood and accepted. It is true that one might assign a value to the use of a compound miter saw; one could simply call a tool rental business and inquire as to how much it would cost to rent such a saw for a specified period. There: value. In dollars and cents.

But the gifting of the saw's use[33] has worth, precisely because, in opting for this exchange between us, Erik and we choose to, in the words of Hyde, *be bothered*. We choose to assume all the responsibility and risk that money abolishes, and therefore we create the possibility of a "feeling-bond" that cannot be sold into the commodity market for a particular value. Now, it could rightly be said that this feeling-bond might not be of the warm and fuzzy sort. For instance, what if Erik had left our saw out in the rain or dropped it from a great height? What if we had neglected to tell him how the safety guard tends to get hung up, rendering it ineffective, and he had inadvertently removed a digit or two with its toothy blade?[34] The term "feeling-bond" has a noble ring to it, but

---

[33] Here is an important point: A loan is a gift of sorts, so long as the money is lent without the expectation of excess repayment. (Still, I'm waiting for that damn beef!)

[34] Come to think of it, we *did* forget to tell him. Although, last time I checked, Erik was still in possession of his full allotment of fingers and thumbs.

of course feelings can be hurt or hard; of course bonds can be broken as well as formed. We should not pretend that these things cannot happen, and we should not be too quick to dismiss the virtue of the commodity economy that Hyde mentions: disconnectedness. And with disconnectedness comes the abjuration of risk.

None of this happened, and so our feeling-bond with Erik, already strong, was strengthened a little more. We were reminded of his responsibility and general conscientiousness when he returned the saw in perfect working order on the agreed-upon date. He was reminded of our generosity and general desire to help when we offered the saw in the first place. If, postloan, he felt some small obligation to us, that sense of indebtedness only strengthened the bond further, and provided yet another opportunity to build upon it.

This arrangement was not unfamiliar to me; indeed, Penny and I had leaned heavily on trust and generosity during the building of our house, although never so heavily or completely as Erik. But for the first time, looking back, I began to reconsider these earlier exchanges, which had done nothing less than put a roof over our heads, in the context of currency. Was it possible that these exchanges and by extension the relationships that enabled them were themselves a form of money? How different were these exchanges, really, for not requiring physical currency to facilitate them? If, per my contention, money is not so much a thing as it is a web of arrangements and unspoken agreements, could Erik's informal exchanges with friends and community be thought of as monetized? After all, he'd gotten what he needed, as he would have if he'd paid in dollars. What did he give up? This seemed harder to define, but there was little doubt in my mind that he gave up *something*, that some small piece of obligation was accrued and that this obligation was, in a sense, credit extended. It was a debt he owed to the owner of the tools, who believed and trusted that Erik was a good credit risk.

When I mentioned this theory to Erik, somewhat to my surprise, he agreed. "In a sense, money is just a representation of trust that if I give you something, you'll give me something back. Sometimes, I think it's trust we're really after, and denominating it in dollars actually trivializes the exchange." We were in his kitchen, noshing on a very nice goat cheese he'd liberated from the dumpster of an artisanal cheese–making outfit,[35] eating it by the heaping spoonful straight from its wrapper.

Erik's belief that trust is a viable form of currency isn't as radical as one might first assume. Obviously, trust is at the core of our contemporary money system, as it must be with any currency, fiat or otherwise. If there is no confidence in the system, there is no confidence in the currency's value, and the whole thing falls apart. Maintaining trust in currency is a crucial aspect of any successful government, if for no other reason than self-preservation, and any government that loses the public's faith in its currency tends to have a decidedly hard time holding on to power. To suggest that the United States' current monetary system is suffering through a crisis of faith isn't exactly going out on a limb, although we have not yet experienced a wholesale abandonment of trust. Nonetheless, it has become increasingly clear that policies and interventions relating to our nation's financial and monetary systems do not benefit us all equally, and it's no surprise that, for those of us consigned to the sour end of the deal, our confidence is waning.

Perhaps the larger issue, however, is the commodity nature of

---

[35] He did this every so often—went dumpster diving for food and other essentials—and the riches he uncovered were astounding in their diversity and simple quality. The price stickers on the wrapper of the cheese we were eating suggested it had sold for $19 per pound, and not long after he'd liberated the goat cheese from the dumpster's dark maw, he showed up at our house with a few sticks of Italian dried sausage, each of which had sold for 12 bucks. He left them with us; I ate a few bites with no small amount of trepidation, but a week later I remained hale and hearty, and so I invited my family to enjoy the remainder of the sausage with me.

money. A dollar is a dollar is a dollar; they are indistinguishable from one another only via careful examination of the green serial numbers printed on each bill. But seriously, have you *ever* looked at those numbers? Of course, credit only extends the characteristic of anonymity, and it's not unreasonable to postulate that the very nature of modern money—its numbing sameness—also both trivializes and commodifies the relationships that form around its exchange. If the value of everything is reduced to monetary units, and if the monetary units used to purchase these items are merely reproduced symbols of a currency that is already fraught with mistrust, is it any wonder that every aspect of the exchanges conducted with these units are imbued with the same hollow sense of value and homogeneity?[36]

In more concrete terms, Erik could have purchased his tools from a hardware store and his building supplies from a lumberyard. He could have hired a contractor to build his cabin, and a plumber to . . . oh, wait: There *wasn't* any plumbing. Still, each of these acts would have hinged on the exchange of money; payment would be made, the goods exchanged, and in the end the resulting relationships of these transactions, by and large, extinguished. Because what money ultimately does is provide a convenient mechanism through which to absolve debt in a very immediate and impersonal way. The dollar I pay to you is exactly the same as the dollar you pay to another; heck it might even *be* the same dollar. This arrangement works only because the value of these dollars is indifferent to—and unaffected by—our personal differences and sense of what something is worth.

---

[36] Now, it is also true that the dollar's homogeneous nature is precisely what lends it ubiquitous value. Indeed, commodity products must by necessity adhere to a common standard or they can't be traded on large-scale commodity markets, lest they suffer a crisis of faith in their value. This is true across practically all market segments, from oil, to corn, to cotton, to cars. We expect even our Big Macs to replicate, and we trust that the recipe for the Special Sauce in a New York City McDonald's is precisely the same recipe that's used in Los Angeles.

We often think of the word "debt" as being strictly financial in nature, but like so many of the words whose definition has been co-opted by the financial realm, that money-based association provides an overly simplistic and incomplete view of things, because, of course, debt can and does arise from human relationships. It can and does exist outside the boundaries of money. When we speak of "owing" favors, we use a vernacular that acknowledges either a debt of service or simple gratitude. In other words, a debt can be as personal or impersonal as the currency we use to make good on it. The impersonality of the dollar (to say nothing of credit) and the efficient, no-strings-attached nature with which it absolves debt are decidedly convenient, and perhaps this is for the good. But when we utilize money, we by default outsource a degree of interpersonal trust and value, instead relying on the homogenized trust and value inherent in the dollar.

Indeed, at every step of Erik's construction process, I saw how mutual trust, combined with no small amount of toil, had built his home. The owner of the property on which he'd built trusted that he would treat the land with respect; he trusted that she wouldn't send him packing or sell the land out from underneath him. Those who loaned him tools trusted that he would return them in good working order on an agreed-upon date. What labor was not the product of his own sweat had been given freely and without a specific expectation of reciprocity. But even this indicated the presence of trust, for there was confidence that Erik would not exploit this generosity and that, if called upon, he in turn would extend it to others in need. These might or might not be the specific individuals who had helped him nail down his siding or plaster his walls; rather, it was as if Erik simply served as the vessel of this trust and giving. He would hold it like a currency, as if he were merely its temporary vessel, to be dispensed into the community as needs dictated.

To the extent possible, Erik gleaned the constituent materials of his cabin: clay from the stream bank; sheep's wool from his friend Bradski; cow manure from my family's small farm.[37] Like the clay, the stones had been hauled from the most-generous stream. Lumber had been purchased from a small, family-run sawmill up the road, and the windows—all used—from a variety of sources.

From these arrangements, numerous benefits could blossom. Of course, one was the manner in which they allowed him—and those with whom he did "commerce"—to reduce their dependence on money and all the attendant issues of how to earn and manage it. Less obvious was the depth of the connections he'd forged with the wide circle of friends and acquaintances that made up his "economy." In the absence of money's depersonalizing element, they were both forced *and* allowed to forge more meaningful connections based on trust and mutual generosity. They were not merely parties to a transaction, but members of an interconnected community that depended on one another in ways that are largely absent from 21st–century first world society.

"To give and receive, to owe and be owed, to depend on others and be depended upon—this is being fully alive. To neither give nor receive, but to pay for everything; to never depend on anyone, but to be financially independent; to not be bound to a community or place, but to be mobile . . . such is the illusory paradise of the discrete and separate self." These are the words of Charles Eisenstein in his groundbreaking book *Sacred Economics*. The "discrete and separate self" Eisenstein speaks of is the contemporary illusion of autonomy from each other and from nature. Eisenstein argues that this disconnect is due in large part to the use of money as an exchange mechanism. When we settle our debts via monetary exchanges, we extinguish any lingering obligation. True, it may at times feel inconvenient or even uncomfortable

[37] Sheep's wool, and cow manure? Really? Read on, for all will be revealed.

to feel indebted to someone, to "owe them a favor." But this discomfort arises only from the illusory wealth of money, which has largely absolved us of the need to rely on others and, likewise, to have them rely on us.

It was through this accounting that I fully and finally began to understand how it was that Erik viewed himself as being not frugal but rather downright rich. Because he views assessments of his prosperity in much the same way he views his economy: as being about more than money. He doesn't have many of the things money can buy, that much is irrefutably true. He has no car, no iPad, no television or cell phone. His life is bereft of anonymous goods, purchased with anonymous dollars, created by hands made anonymous by distance and cultural divides. In this regard, he is poor and, to the extent that one views these goods as desirable and even essential, perhaps even pitiable.

But the more time I spent with Erik, the better I understood that any measure of prosperity based on the compiling of generic goods, no matter how technologically alluring or promising of convenience and comfort, was at best an example of half-done math. The world is awash in these homogenized items; the prosperity that comes of owning them is a homogenized prosperity, no amount of which can fill that void that comes of the disquieting realization that perhaps *we* are becoming homogenous, too.

The allure of these manufactured goods is built on story after story. First, and almost always, the once-upon-a-time story that they will somehow free us to live the life we truly want to live, a life that always seems just beyond our reach, like the rainbow's end, or the proverbial carrot on a stick. Often, this story is rooted in the premise that contemporary technological marvels—faster computers, talking cell phones, wireless freakin' everything—will not only simplify our lives, leaving us with more free time to spend with loved ones or engage in the leisure time activity of our choosing, but will usher in a new era of abundance for all. Increasingly, however, the leisure time activity of our choosing seems to be engaging with the very technological marvels that promise more leisure time. In 2010, Americans set a record for television watching, at 34 hours per week; that same year, a study by the Kaiser Family Foundation revealed that teenagers spent 53 hours each week immersed in digital media. A new generation is already on the hook.

In their *New York Times* best-selling book *Abundance: The Future Is Better than You Think*, Peter Diamandis and Steven Kotler repeat the tired refrain that technology is poised to somehow do what it has time and again proven incapable of doing: lift all boats.

> There are the very poorest of the poor, the so-called bottom billion, who are finally plugging into the global economy and are poised to become what I call "the rising billion." The creation of the global transportation network was the initial step down this path, but it's the combination of the Internet, microfinance, and wireless communication technology that's transforming the poorest of the poor into an emerging market force. Acting alone, each of these three forces has enormous potential. But acting together, amplified by exponentially growing technologies, the once-unimaginable becomes the now actually possible.

It's a seductive notion, I'll give them that, but if the current state of income and asset wealth inequality on both national and global scales hasn't put to rest the notion that digitized technology cannot and will not be a vector for ubiquitous prosperity, it's hard to image what will finally expose this sham for what it is: a thinly veiled "opportunity" for industry to continue producing and selling us stuff we don't need. Diamandis and Kotler's rosy assessment even hints at such, as evidenced by the phrase: "transform the poorest of the poor into an emerging market force." Of course, this is the sad and self-centered language of the unconscious economy, in its tireless quest to convert us into a world of consumers.

The second story told by the allure of homogenized products that proliferate in 21st-century markets is even more ironic: that they are precisely the opposite of homogenous, providing a blank canvas on which we might express our individuality. The consumer marketplace is awash with examples: IKEA suggests we "customize" our homes, via the purchase and installation of their assembly-line particleboard wares, which the company churns out in great confidence by the millions, having utilized extensive market research to determine what designs and features are most likely to appeal to the greatest number of consumers. And Apple, a company founded on the notion of creative individualism ("think different"), brings us the ethereal, digitized Siri, whose engineered voice sounds as if the poor girl is being whacked on the head repeatedly as she speaks.

With Siri, even our conversations can be homogenized. After watching an Apple-produced online video touting her robotic charms, I found myself wondering if perhaps I'd stumbled across a parody. What I saw was both disturbing and, it must be said, rather hilarious, if only for its pathos: well-groomed thirty-somethings talking to their telephones and then patiently awaiting Siri's stilted reply. Here is an actual "conversation" from the video I viewed:

SIRI: New notification for messages. Sandy Cheng. Are we still on for. Dinner to. Night?
WELL-GROOMED THIRTY-SOMETHING: Reply: Sure, I'll be there.
SIRI: Here's your reply to Sandy Cheng: Sure. I'll be. There.
WGTS (SMILING): Send.

Are you kidding me?!? *This* is progress? *This* is what folks camped out on sidewalks for? So they could be among the first to tell a machine what to tell a person, and then listen back to what they told "her" to tell that person, before telling "her" to actually go ahead and tell that person what they wish to tell them? Are we truly so lacking in reverence for one another that we wish for our relationships to be mediated by a computer-generated entity that, no matter what it's saying and to whom, sounds Pre. Cisely the same? Siri is the Special Sauce of communication: predictable, hollowly satisfying, and never deviating from the standard. She represents the antithesis of individuality and autonomy.[38]

In contrast, practically everything Erik surrounds himself with—his wealth—was anything but homogeneous. It is rooted in personal relationship, trust, and face-to-face communications. It isn't that he eschews technology in its entirety; hell, he even has an e-mail account, though he doesn't seem to use it much. But he has contracted neither his wealth nor his relationships (which of course are a constituent part of his wealth) to entities beyond the reach of his control. There is very little in his life that can be made obsolete by a new model; his wealth is largely independent of policy and world affairs over which he has little bearing. This explains in large part why he'd been able to remain so sanguine throughout the 2008 financial crisis: It simply wasn't part of his world, at least not to the extent that it was and still is for most Americans.

This is not to suggest that Erik is accountable to nothing. It's just that the things he *is* accountable to remain primarily within his sphere of influence. His prosperity demands that he uphold his end of multiple unspoken agreements that backstop the exchanges that make his life work; it demands responsibility and accountability and he accepts these things willingly, not just because he has to, but also because he *wants* to. Because—surprise, surprise—it actually feels good to take responsibility, not only for ourselves, but for one another.

---

[38]It is not that technology is inherently problematic; it is that, like money itself, we have allowed technology to exceed appropriate boundaries to the point where it does not merely enhance our lives and connections with others, but defines them.

Over the past century or so, and perhaps longer, we have been taught that to rely on others is to be weak and incapable. The notion that we should be dependent on one another is almost antithetical to contemporary American expectations of autonomy and independence. But in truth it is that autonomy that exploits and, irony of ironies, turns us all into dependents of the very arrangements that profess to offer independence. It exploits our resource base, because it depends on each of us owning the raw materials that enable us to shun one another. But even more profoundly, it exploits *us*, because it deprives us of the opportunity to experience the richness of interconnectedness and the meaningful relationships it gives rise to. By striving to achieve the American ideal of personal independence, we wind up not just independent, but isolated.

I could see now how completely I'd placed everything out of order. I'd long thought that Erik's enviable contentment was the result, somehow, of his eschewing money. A symptom of his poverty, if you will. But now I saw that his monetary poverty was itself a symptom of his having chosen, in fact, an accumulation of wealth that could never be measured in mere dollars, and that furthermore, his contentment arose from a deeper well of prosperity than I'd ever imagined. It was almost as if money was irrelevant to his well-being; he might have money, he might not, but either way, it didn't really matter all that much.[39]

In fact, I was beginning to grasp just how profoundly Erik's wealth was not the result of shunning money, or anything else, really. Indeed, it was precisely the opposite: the inevitable result of *embracing* that which filled his life with happiness. Of course, this was coupled with the wisdom to differentiate between the hollow, fleeting gratifications offered by the commodity marketplace and

---

[39] I say "almost" because, as I've repeatedly pointed out, Erik *does* need money. He just needs it a whole heck of a lot less than most of us.

the durable, if occasionally inconvenient, satisfaction to which both Eisenstein and Hyde refer.

In simplest terms, Erik was content not because he was poor, but because he was *alive.* And just as it is naïve to believe that the accumulation of money and commodity assets can buy happiness, it is equally misguided to assume that the *nonaccumulation* of these things will deliver true wealth. One can simply shun money and be poor if one does not embrace a life that seeks to exchange value for worth.

In other words, it wasn't so much that I needed to cut back on what I already had; it was that I needed to embrace that which I *didn't.* And no amount of money—either lesser or greater—could help make this happen.

[CHAPTER NINE]

In which I have doubts.

ON THE last day of November 2011, almost exactly a year after my initial visit to Erik's cabin, I returned to the structure. It wasn't the first time I'd visited since the previous November, but it was notable for numerous reasons. For one, it had been the second-warmest autumn on record, and the day was almost freakishly balmy. A few stubborn patches of slush lay in the wooded, north-facing shadows, the week-old remnants of a storm that had dropped nearly a foot of wet snow. But that event had been anomalous, and a string of 50°F and 60°F days had quickly erased all but the most passing evidence that it had happened at all. Still, there was another, more consequential reason that this visit was so different from the one a year before: Erik no longer lived in his house. Inaeed, it seemed that the circumstances of his life had changed rather dramatically in just a few short months.

Most profoundly, his girlfriend, Heidi, had found a house she wished to purchase. This had happened in a manner so unscripted, so counter to the way most Americans go about achieving these sorts of milestones, that I couldn't help but feel as if she had somehow been fated to inhabit this particular, and no other, home. To begin, the house she found hadn't even been for sale, a basic prerequisite of eligibility that had not deterred Heidi in the least. Instead, she'd simply knocked on the weather-beaten front door and stated her keen interest in purchasing the place if the owner ever decided to sell. I suspect that even Heidi thought she'd be turned away, but such was not the case: "You know," said the owner, "perhaps I *would* like to sell."

There were still some kinks to work out, chief among them that Heidi had no credit history (a few years before, she'd procured a Visa card in order to establish her creditworthiness but had found using it distasteful and had abandoned it before any pattern of repayment had been established). So for the time being, while the bank figured out what to do with her, Heidi was renting the house, and Erik had moved in with her. So too had Erik's younger brother, Ryan, who'd graduated from Saint Lawrence University in the spring and had come to Vermont to consider his future.

The house was small, and humbly funky, with lots of exposed wood, both inside and out. There was nothing to hide where this house had come from; everything whispered of its origins. The unpainted wood looked, well, like wood, and if one were to run fingers over the rough surface of, say, the house's siding or its window trim, the boards actually felt like a tree beneath the fingers. Heck, the place even *smelled* like a tree. There were cracks and gaps everywhere, including between the upstairs floorboards, so that anything spilled might drip down onto the heads of those below.

The house sat on 2½ acres, pushed against a steep, forested hillside, into which a root cellar would be dug and, perhaps, a few pigs would be kept. There was a garden, and a listing outbuilding, and small parking area for Heidi's little Toyota pickup and the old station wagon that Ryan had purchased and to which Erik had been granted seemingly unrestricted access. I'd been surprised, the first time I'd ridden as a passenger in the car, at how heedlessly Erik drove. But then I realized he was merely allowing the car to generate as much momentum on the descents as possible, so that he might slingshot up the next rise using the minimum amount of fuel. Still, the first time I rode with him he misjudged the car's braking power relative to a looming stop sign, and we'd skidded to a screeching halt. This version of Erik, stomping on the brake pedal so willfully as to leave four thick black strips of rubber on the tarmac, was so opposed to my entrenched view of him as a man who conducted himself with utter mindfulness, with the utmost respect for the natural world, that I'd nearly broken into laughter, forgetting for a moment that he'd almost blasted into a busy intersection.

So yes, Heidi's house was small and funky (although nowhere near as small as Erik's cabin, and nowhere near as funky as the rental he'd inhabited before building his place), but it still represented a fairly significant vertical rise in Erik's standard of living. He hadn't climbed a mere single rung on the ladder; he'd skipped over a good three or four, to a vantage point that offered an exquisite view of life with electricity, a flush toilet, and refrigeration. They were even shopping for a chest freezer, albeit a used one. There was rent to pay and, assuming Heidi could navigate the lending process, there would soon be a mortgage to service ("death pledge" is what Erik repeatedly called it, referring to the original French law meaning of the word, an apparent reference to the fact that the agreement dies only when the obligation is fulfilled or the property is foreclosed on), along with the requisite homeowner's insurance and annual property tax bill. Erik still didn't own a car of his own, of course, but between Heidi's truck and Ryan's little runabout, he may as well have.

Did Erik's sudden and significant leap to an exponentially higher standard of living give me pause? Well, yes, and quite reasonably so, I'd argue. For despite my recognition that Erik's wealth was not dependent on his thrift, or on his having eschewed the trappings of contemporary American life, how could I not wonder if perhaps he had allowed himself to become swept downstream by the very current he'd spent the majority of his adult life swimming against? How could I not wonder if he'd capitulated, if he'd simply grown weary of living within the self-imposed boundaries of his self-imposed thrift? How could I not wonder if he'd followed a path similar to my parents' and abandoned the simple life for the easy one? From all outward appearances, I certainly couldn't dismiss the possibility that the man had given in to the status quo. From the outset of my friendship with him, I'd always seen Erik's housing—and in particular, the manner in which he'd built his own home—as somehow emblematic of his relationship to money and wealth. Now, and rather suddenly, the particulars of his shelter had changed dramatically, and I could not help but wonder what else might change too.

Yet, in my more charitable moments, I decided that maybe he'd merely bowed to the same fate that has befallen so many of humanity's best intentions: love. After all, it wasn't Erik who knocked on the door of the weathered little cape; it was Heidi. It wasn't Erik who was trying to convince the bank to extend a loan to someone who had a meager repayment history; it was Heidi. Maybe it was as simple as this: Erik had followed the girl he loved to the home she wished to buy. Rather begrudgingly, I had to admit that I would have done exactly the same, and under the circumstances, his upward mobility seemed entirely justified.

This was something of a conundrum for me because I suddenly had the nagging sense that perhaps I had overestimated his commitment to thrift. Worse yet, this was followed by the even more nagging sense that the very thesis on which I'd built my book was imperiled. Who was I to blame for that, assuming it was not myself? Heidi? That hardly seemed fair. Besides, the notion of blaming anything on this sweetly soft-spoken young woman, with her omnipotent cheer and midwestern warmth, made me feel like an ogre. So, Erik was out, Heidi was out, and I lacked the introspection (or maybe it was simple courage I lacked) to blame myself. One option remained: hope like hell that Erik's new living quarters were somehow immaterial to his ethos of thrift.

This may all seem a bit dramatic. But for more than a year I'd viewed Erik as a mentor to my evolving understanding of money and wealth. And of all the facets that had originally drawn me to him, his exceptional contentment with the humble shelter he was building for himself was most affecting. Given this context, how could I not be alarmed that he'd suddenly abandoned his modest home? And this alarm, at least in part, explained my return to his cabin on this preternaturally warm November day: I hoped, quite frankly, to dispel my concerns. I hadn't seen much of Erik in the past few weeks, and I was wondering if perhaps all I needed to regain my confidence was to immerse myself in his life again, even for a few short hours.

I met Erik at the new place, where he, Heidi, and a young, twenty-something, shaggy-haired fellow named Sepke (Sespe? Kepse?) were all tucking into a tin of warm muffins. The plan for the morning, once everyone had had their fill of muffin, was to head over to the cabin, where Erik was midway through an application of finish plaster on the interior walls. Over the preceding year, he'd made slow-but-steady progress on the place, which, now that he was living at Heidi's, he had begun to refer to as his "mancave." He'd finished the exterior siding and installed a front door; more significantly, he'd insulated the walls with a combination of clay, water, straw, and little chopped-up bits of Styrofoam, which he'd gotten somewhere for free and felt compelled to use, despite the fact that it didn't really fit the earthy ethos of the place. The mixture was, essentially, muck, peppered with little blue chunks of polystyrene, and he'd scooped and packed it into the wall cavities behind thin strips of wooden lath to hold it in place. Once the insulation dried sufficiently, he'd smear thin layers of the plaster concoction over the whole shebang. Muck on muck, if you will. It was not a technique likely to find its way into the pages of *Fine Homebuilding* magazine or *Architectural Digest*, but the price was right, and, if Erik was to be believed, it would deliver performance superior to synthetic insulations and wall coverings. "Contemporary materials aren't evil, but they embody a mindset of working against the place we live," he told me. "This plaster is made of the land from here. It's of this place! And in that sense, it has the capacity to work *with* the place," he explained, emphasizing the word "with."

Before we could head to the cabin, Erik had to make a quick stop en route, so that he might procure a small quantity of sheep's wool, an essential component to the plaster mix, which also contained clay (dug from the stream bank about 20 feet to the south of Erik's front door), sand (sourced from an elderly fellow who, as Erik explained it, spent his spare time swinging his homemade steel club to whack golf balls off a homemade golf tee, made from a modified spark plug no less, into his—you guessed it—homemade sandpit), water (from the same stream that provided the clay), limestone (from the same fellow who had the wool), and cow poop. The manure, Erik explained, was rich in enzymes that would help bind these disparate materials to one another, creating a finish of exceptional durability. I was well past the point of being shocked at much of anything Erik did, and even his smearing cow feces on his walls was no exception.

We piled into Ryan's car and Erik pointed the wagon up a steep hill that led out of town, and within only 2 minutes we had parked and were strolling down a narrow footpath that wound through a field. We passed a large fenced-in garden, climbed a short hill that led to a small, sloping apple orchard, and just beyond, partially obscured by a copse of young pine trees, we caught sight of a clapboarded cabin that was perhaps 10 feet by 12 feet. There was something distinctly fairy tale and even dream-like about the whole scene: The long, trod path, the grassy rise of earth, the wending through the apple trees, and the diminutive nature of the building all created an aura of hazy enchantment, a subtle "through the looking glass" feel.

This was the home of Erik's friend Brad (Erik called him "Bradski"), and although it was nearer to completion than Erik's cabin and assembled with an evident degree of skill that my friend, quite frankly, lacked, it shared much in common with Erik's humble abode. Most obviously similar was its size, or lack thereof, and the fact that there was no electrical service or running water. Less obviously, Bradski's cabin, like Erik's, was situated on land to which he held no title. Sure, he had verbal permission to build there, but still I was struck by the reservoir of trust such an arrangement necessitated. What if his relationship with the property owners took a wrong turn? What if they sold, or lost jobs and were forced into foreclosure? Bradski had obviously invested hundreds of hours into his home; this was no cobbled-together hovel. The frame was hewn of small timbers and the floors sanded and shellacked to a warm sheen. Outside, a dry-stacked stone wall, itself representative of days, if not weeks, of hard and exacting labor, sat half-completed.

We stood in the house for a half-hour or so, chatting. No one seemed in any hurry to get on with the day, despite the fact that it was approaching 10 o'clock. Bradski's girlfriend was curled into the corner of a bench seat, knitting. Far as I could tell, there was no job anyone needed to get to anytime soon, and when Erik asked Bradski when he was expected at his place of work (a bakery), he scrunched his face quizzically, as if scanning his memory for whatever commitment he'd made to his employer. "The seventh," he said, finally. More than a week away.

Finally, we left Bradski's, one small box of wool and a trio of borrowed trowels richer. Despite this being only the first time Sespe (yes, that was it, definitely—I think) had met Bradski and his girlfriend, he embraced them both, and we passed again under the dormant apple trees and over the short rise, where I turned to briefly survey the scene below me. What was it about the view that made me feel as if I could finally exhale a breath I'd been holding for too long? Some of it was aesthetic, I knew. The tidiness, everything so small and tucked into place and even more so, it seemed, being not imposed upon the place but rather *of* it, like the cow feces–enhanced plaster we were about to spread on Erik's walls. It felt somehow *manageable* in a way I'd never experienced at my own home, which, the more I hung out with Erik and the people he brought me into contact with, was beginning to feel like a sprawling embarrassment of riches. The orchard certainly didn't hurt, and along with the setback from the road and the fact that the cabin was accessible only by foot, I had the distinct impression that I'd somehow stumbled upon it in a fateful manner that lacked any definable intent. Again I had the now-familiar sensation that meeting Erik and being drawn into his extended network of like-minded *frugalistas* was one of those serendipitous events that would shape my life in heretofore unimagined ways.

We rolled back down the steep hill and hung a left onto Erik's road. Erik parked and we made our way up the path, which had been significantly affected by Hurricane Irene. The quiet stream that normally burbled alongside the cabin had become a raging torrent, overspilling its banks and diverting much of its flow across Erik's footpath. It was still passable, but the erosion was significant and lent the place a gentle postapocalyptic vibe. Still, there'd been one unexpected fringe benefit of the flooding: It had caused the stream's banks to slide, exposing a large cache of steel-colored clay. It was the very source of the clay we were about to spread on Erik's walls.

Between the visit to Bradski's and the particulars of the interior finish Erik had chosen, the ingredients of which had cost him essentially nothing, I was beginning to regain my faith in my friend's commitment to limited-cash living. This put me in a magnanimous frame of mind, and regarding the move to Heidi's new home, I felt only empathy. Love is a powerful thing, and if it came with the burden of hot running water, a flush toilet, and electrical outlets, well, hey. A guy can make compromises. A fellow can survive these things and so, it seemed to me, can his embrace of extreme thrift.

If anything, Erik's commitment to commodity economy resistance seemed more fervent than ever, and it occurred to me that his recent immersion into relative abundance had only affirmed his desire to live a Spartan existence, in the manner that people sick with a hangover tend to swear off drinking the morning after a binge. It was clear that Erik had been doing a lot of thinking about his chosen lifestyle. Furthermore, he told me, he was questioning if he was doing enough to bring about the changes he wished for the broader world. Why, just the night before, he'd found himself walking the somnolent streets of the neighborhood at 1 o'clock in the morning, his mind wild with thoughts and self-recriminations. This was not the first time he'd been kept awake by his doubts and concerns, he told me. "The question of how to save the planet from industrial crapitalism and disturbia is a question I consider to be lifelong." Erik often employed wordplay when discussing systemic forces he reviled; I wondered if perhaps it was something of a coping mechanism. "It's a question I'm willing to devote my life to. It's crucial, sacred, and incredibly urgent. It is perhaps the thing I feel most beholden to."

Erik could not help but ask himself if it was enough to live a life of conscious-but-quiet intent. Was it enough to create a lifestyle that to the greatest extent possible ensured his nonparticipation in a parasitic system that brings only sorrow and sickness to the natural world and to so many of his fellow Americans, trapped on the majority side of the 99-to-1 percent divide? What actions or nonactions could match the urgency of such a planetary crisis? Was it enough to protest through what he *didn't* do?

"I mediate a lot of my experiences through a judgment: 'Is this the way I want to live my life?'" he told me, as we troweled thin coats of plaster onto the walls. The smell was moist, even dank, like a basement, but it was not unpleasant. "My fear is that I'm just part of a subculture and that a subculture isn't going to slow anything down. I mean, just by building this house and having it be what it is"—I understood that he meant the humble nature of the place, the what-it-is-not as much as the what-it-is—"isn't really going to change anything. It's not going to keep the machine at bay."

I'd long understood that Erik's anticonsumer ethos was rooted in more than the fringe benefits of the freedom it bestowed upon him, and in more than the relationships and skills it fostered. But I'd underestimated how troubled he was by forces that felt beyond his control, forces that would not be defeated by his having chosen to live on the margins. He was but 1-in-300-million-odd Americans. In terms of shifting the status quo, the numbers were not on his side.

He continued: "The industrial economy wants us to believe that our choices are limited to what we can buy, and that what we buy is how we define our lifestyle." The conundrum, of course, was that defining a lifestyle by choosing *not* to buy was still defining a lifestyle, and Erik was beginning to wonder if lifestyle alone could affect the sort of change he knew in his heart was essential.

"I wish I could just live a kick-ass life connected to the land," he said later, when we paused to gnaw on some carrots I'd brought along for a snack. "I mean, some people drop out and live in a sweet little straw-bale house in the woods. . . ." His voice trailed off, and he looked a little pained, as if he wanted to want nothing more than to want nothing more than that, the simple satisfaction derived of starving the system as much as any one person can starve the system of its lifeblood: money. From a material standpoint, he was fulfilled. To be sure, this fulfillment was based on a laughably meager collection of belongings, at least when compared to our culture at large. Still, there was little doubt in my mind that his was true fulfillment in this regard, and probably even truer than most of us realize in our personal lives.

But Erik had bumped up against the same wall that many of us bump up against at some point: You can't buy contentment. Perhaps more accurately, he'd bumped up against the other side of that very same wall: You can't *not* buy contentment. It wasn't that he was overtly unhappy—indeed, I still viewed him as one of the happiest, most content people I knew—but there was nonetheless something gnawing at him, and its teeth were becoming harder to ignore, in part because the beast was no longer satisfied with being fed on Erik's nonparticipation in the moneyed economy. Erik had reached one of those inflection points that all of us reach at different times in our lives, where it seemed as if the particulars of his future should be determined not by choices that were hard and specific and evidenced by a single action, but by subtler choices of an evolving ethos and the multiple actions that would dictate.

He wanted to want only what he already had, but something inside of him was whispering, *It's not enough, it's not enough.* To a man who for most of his adult life had defined himself by setting his expectations of "enough" so low that a 96-square-foot house was both a source of unbridled joy and no small amount of pride, this incessant whisper must have been confusing. *It's not enough, it's not enough.* He'd done everything he knew how to do, he'd scrounged and scraped and downright willed himself out of the machine. What more, really, could he do?

"I think I have to go beyond the lifestyle," he said, as he tossed his carrot end into the woods and reached for his trowel.

"So then you have to decide what that means and how to act on it," I pointed out, which probably doesn't rank very high on my all-time list of Most Helpful Things I've Ever Said.

He chuckled, but it was rueful, not humorous. "That's why I was up all night."

Then he grabbed a handful of plaster, smacked it against the wall, and leaned into his trowel.

[CHAPTER TEN]

In which I choose freedom.

IN LATE February, Erik called to see if I wanted to go skiing the next day. I did not have to ask if he meant alpine skiing; the idea of Erik driving an hour and paying $70 for the privilege of being carried to the mountain's summit, so that he might slide back down atop a veneer of man-made snow, was preposterous. It was like imagining the pope in Pizza Hut. Nothing about it fit.

Still, the notion of cross-country skiing seemed to me nearly as unlikely, if only because the ground was all but devoid of snow. It had been the sort of winter that could compel even the most right-wing ideologue to embrace the concept of anthropogenic climate change; the average temperature for January had been a full 6°F warmer than normal, and snowfall was nearing historic lows. The passing storms had delivered mostly rain or, on rare occasions when the thermometer dropped below freezing, a dispiriting spittlelike substance that encased everything in a rind of ice. By the middle of February, nearly 3 weeks ahead of the historical schedule, almost all the state's commercial syrup makers had set their taps, and some were already boiling. Great billows of steam rose from the rooftop vents affixed atop the sugarhouses. If you were lucky, you could catch a whiff of hot syrup as you passed.

Befitting the winter's general temperament, the day I drove to Erik's with my long-neglected skis in my car was warm and glowering. It was precipitating lightly, and I say "precipitating" because none of the usual descriptors seem apt. It was not snow. Nor was it rain, or sleet. It was definitely not hail, although it made a spattering sound on my windshield, before half-bouncing, half-sliding down the glass. It was not shaping up to be a pleasant day.

It was about 8:30 on a Thursday morning when I embarked, perhaps a little late for the morning work rush, but not so late that there wasn't plenty of traffic, particularly in the westbound lane, which led toward the state's centers of commerce. Not for the first time, I was struck by the freedom Erik had forged for himself, and, for a moment, I allowed myself to feel pleased that I too was free to do as I wished at a time when most Americans were heading to jobs that the majority found unfulfilling. True, I was, in effect, getting paid to ski with Erik, to the extent that time spent with him could be considered "research." In short, I was going to work too. This was actually an uplifting realization for me; I recalled Erik's quandary over whether or not to spend $675 on a secondhand bicycle, and how he'd decided the enjoyment he'd glean from the bike was entirely worth the time he'd given to earn the money.

Ah, money. It had been on my mind of late because, much to my consternation, things were a little tight. Not threateningly so, but a recent spate of car trouble had cut a pretty wide swath through our modest savings, and I worried that it would not be replenished before something else broke. Of late, I had found myself obsessing over our finances, not quite able to convince myself that everything was going to work itself out. This was humbling to me, for it revealed the weak links of my assumptions regarding monetary wealth: namely, that while money can serve as our master it can also serve as our liberator. Suddenly, my entire thesis—that the accumulation of money beyond our immediate needs demeans and impoverishes us—felt a bit shaky. Because what I really wanted at the moment, if I'm to be entirely frank, was a bit more dough.

As it turns out, Heidi's truck had also broken recently, in a fairly catastrophic way that suggested its next journey might be on the back of a flatbed, bound for the nearest scrapyard. No one seemed in any hurry to resolve the situation, however, and so for now it sat forlornly in the driveway, awaiting its fate. I parked near it, but not too near, in case whatever affliction had felled it was contagious.

Erik stowed his battered skis in the back of my Subaru and directed me up the same hill we'd driven nearly a year before, on our way to liberating a dozen or so pounds of morels from the forest floor. He wore wool pants, a wool sweater, a wool sweater vest, and a wool hat. I'd no doubt his socks were also wool and that if he wore underwear, it was the product of the sheep species. All his visible wool garments were frayed at the edges, suggesting years of use. There was large smudge of soot on the side of his nose; it curled around and disappeared into his left nostril. I considered mentioning it to him, but realized he wouldn't care; it had long been obvious to me that Erik placed minimal stock in his physical appearance.

As we climbed out of town, the patches of bare soil between the islands of snow began to shrink, and soon the ground was white . . . almost. It was not the soft, pure white of a cold winter's day; instead, it was dingy and almost gray, possessing a granularity that did not look very inviting. But at least it was snow. Earlier in the day, I'd doubted the conditions would enable us to ski, but of course Erik had known differently. He'd known where the snow would be.

We nosed up a dirt road, barely wide enough to accommodate a single vehicle. My car sputtered worryingly. "I used to live in a real sweet cabin up here," Erik said, and for a moment I became confused and a little disoriented: Was it the same cabin we'd stumbled upon during our mushroom hunt? Erik chuckled. "No, no. A different one." The road dead-ended into a misshapen snow bank, and we disembarked. We strapped on our skis, then glided into the woods on an abandoned logging road. I could see the parallel indentations of an older ski track, faded by a few days of above-freezing temperatures. I pointed to the tracks with my eyebrows raised; Erik nodded. They were his.

Soon, the logging road began to climb, and shortly thereafter, I fell in behind Erik. Shortly after that, a distance opened between us, small at first, but growing to become considerable. I huffed and sweated and paused a moment to gather myself; Erik shuffled on with apparent ease, his body tuned to the rigors of self-propulsion. It was a little dispiriting, but then, I'd expected it, remembering how effortlessly he strode up the mountain the previous May. Before long, Erik cast a glance over his shoulder, saw that I'd been spit into the distance, and pulled up. For the rest of our outing, he checked his speed and we skied in sync.

Toward the top of the hill, Erik veered from the logging road and I followed. Away from the cleared path, the forest was dense and we picked our way through the meager openings between trees, mostly maple, but also some ash and yellow birch. A rough branch scraped hard across my cheek, and I paused to pull off a glove and place my fingers to the wound. A red drop. I flicked it to the ground, and the crimson dot spread as it melted into the surrounding snow.

We crossed the tracks of a moose, pressed deep and still crisp at the edges, only hours old. After a few hundred feet, the forest began to thin a little and then, rather abruptly, we came to a wall of stone. It was maybe 3 feet high, and assembled from roundish specimens, some small and manageable by human strength; others large and beyond the capacity of any man or woman, no matter their stature or will. The stones were various hues of gray and brown, and many had tumbled from where they had been perched decades or even centuries before.

I gazed along the line formed by the wall, which ran in both directions as far as I could see. So many rocks, so much toil, and I thought immediately of the Yapese, who'd used stone as currency. To gather their money, they'd frequently traveled to distant islands, where they'd quarried the stones and then rafted them home behind canoes. It sounds absurd, crazy even. But of course it's no different from what happens with gold, which holds value simply because we decide it should.[40] And it's hardly different from paper money, minus the devastation wrought by mining and processing. I wondered for a moment about the feasibility of using a stone wall as currency. Hey, if the Yapese could do it. . . .

Erik broke the silence. "I'm really curious: How long did it take to build a wall like this?" He rested a bare hand atop it, as if feeling the stone against his palm might somehow give him a sense of what had gone into the wall's construction. I reached out, too; it was cold, rough. It felt old. Erik was quiet for a moment, and then: "It's kind of cool to think about the soil under this wall. I wonder how different it is. . . . I mean, it's been under there for all these years."

I nodded but did not say anything, primarily because I did not know what to say. Maybe Erik's observation meant little; maybe it

---

[40] It's worth pointing out that gold *does* have industrial value, primarily in electronics. But this accounts for only a fraction of world supply; the vast majority is made into jewelry or held as a store of wealth, and it is these uses that largely determine the price of gold.

was nothing more than the musings of a man whose observations had a tendency to fall far outside the boundaries of the contemporary American experience, for try as I might, I could not think of anyone else who would come across a tumbledown stone wall deep in the woods of rural Vermont and wonder about the soil lying beneath it, and it occurred to me that perhaps this meant nothing more than that Erik was a little nuts.

But if Erik was nuts, what did that say about me and my own musings on the value of stone? Suddenly, I felt a bit—no, not merely a bit: a lot—silly for having allowed myself to wallow in such senselessness. Here I was, with a barely running 18-year-old car, an even older, even more barely running truck, and a severely depleted savings account, and I was hanging out in the woods, thinking about the value of a freakin' stone wall? I was spending my day—this small bit of my *life*—skiing over a barely skiable crust of granular snow with a man who saw fit to ponder a patch of soil he would never see? I mean, really: What the hell was wrong with me? I should be home, at my desk, chasing work that, even if it weren't entirely meaningful, would at least generate the income I so desperately needed to provide for myself and my family, conscious economy or no.

Yet despite my misgivings and sudden crisis of confidence, I suspected there was a deeper truth lurking in Erik's curiosity, and I wondered if it was this: Most of us have aligned ourselves so thoroughly with the unconscious economy that it has occupied us not only physically, but also emotionally and intellectually. To pause to consider the history of a wall, or the state of the soil beneath it, strikes me as a bit crazy only because I cannot articulate any rational justification for doing so. But of course the parameters for what I deemed "rational" had long ago been set by the unconscious economy, in which so many of my actions *and* thoughts were oriented around the business of making and managing money.

For the first time, I considered how it was that Erik's indifferent relationship to money freed him not just physically, but *intellectually*. In other words, it wasn't merely time (life) he gained by reducing his reliance on money to a bare minimum; it was also the capacity to *think* for himself, simply because so few of his waking hours were consumed by either the task of earning or thinking about money. Try as we might (and I've tried), we are capable of but one thought at a time, which means that time spent dwelling on matters of finance is by default time not spent thinking about, well, much of anything else. We tend to think of freedom in the context of flesh and blood, but of course our thoughts can be shackled too, and this explains, in part, why I could not help questioning the value of standing beside a pile of stones in the middle of February and considering what lay beneath it, or how and why it had been constructed. My body was free. My mind was not. I had given myself only half a gift.

How often, I wondered, do we deny ourselves these gifts, much in the same way we deny ourselves the pleasure of offering our gifts to others, be they intellectual, artistic, or of pure toil? *I can't afford that*, we say, and we believe it, because we inhabit the unconscious economy where everything, not least our time, has value, rather than worth.[41] It is not hard to understand why this view is seductive; as Lewis Hyde so poetically points out in *The Gift*: "The excitement of commodities is the excitement of possibility, of floating away from the particular to taste the range of available life. There are times when we want to be aliens and strangers, to feel

---

[41] This is not to say there is no overlap between "value" and "worth," or that both cannot be peacefully embodied by the same object or experience. Consider Erik's bicycle, which he'd purchased at a fixed price (value) and which could be resold for particular price (value), but which also represented to him the sum total of all his experiences aboard it (worth), as well as the manner in which he earned the money necessary to assume its possession (value *and* worth).

how the shape of our lives is not the only shape, to drift before a catalog of possible lives, staring at the glass arcades of shoes that are sensible and shoes for taking a chance, buses leaving town and the gray steam railway depot where men and women hurry by with their bags."

In other words, the autonomy and faux-individualism offered by the unconscious economy may well be undermining our true wealth—they may well be driving wedges between us and also between humanity and the natural world, keeping us from offering our true gifts to the world and even to ourselves. But damned if doesn't *feel* good to avail ourselves of all the easy choices we are offered, the impacts of which remain invisible to us through the prism of distance and dilution. The world is so vast and resilient, it offers the illusion of absorbing the ramifications of the unconscious economy. But of course there is a point of saturation, and, in so many regards, we seem to have reached that point.

Erik and I skied on, and once I was moving again, I felt better. Lighter. Nothing had changed, really: My car was still in poor repair, and my bank account wasn't doing much better. I had paying work, but only just enough to meet my family's ongoing needs, and there seemed to be no immediate prospect of evading my need for money by acquiring more money. I would need to be resourceful, but I'd done that before and could do it again. We fell into the rhythm of skiing, our arms pistoning forward and back, forward and back, our skis sliding over the snow, reluctant at the onset of each stride, but then overcoming some law of friction that I will never understand, to glide effortlessly over the ground.

We reached the top of a long climb and then turned the tips of our skis to face downhill; a logging road lay before us, curving through the forest, as if following a path laid by an unfurling ball of twine. I pushed off first, and soon found myself achieving a precarious velocity. I heard Erik push off behind me.

At once I whooped. It was an act so spontaneous and uncalculated even I was surprised by the ring of my voice, and as it came I had the strangest thought: Lewis Hyde described the excitement of commodities as the excitement of possibility, of "floating away from the particular to taste the range of available life." But why should we allow the range of available life to be defined by the commodity marketplace? Could it not include two men, on a late winter's day, careening down a logging road on their skis, riding the ragged edge of control? Could it not include wondering about the soil under a stone wall?

Commodities—and the money required to procure them—offer us one view of the possible. Or maybe it is multiple views, all connected and defined on some level by the unconscious economy. Indeed, it is fair to say that for most of us, our lives, relationships, and even our *thoughts* have come to be dominated by the unconscious economy, which we believe offers the "range of available life," as if anything and everything worth experiencing can somehow be priced and marketed. We know this is not true, and yet we are barraged by messages insisting that even the path to those experiences that lie outside the commodity marketplace is paved by the procurement of those very commodities. Consider the notorious MasterCard "priceless" advertising campaign, whereby the realization of that priceless moment, the Holy Grail of what we know to be the richest of human experience, comes only after the acquisition of multiple commodity products, all conveniently charged to our credit cards.

Lewis Hyde is clearly not articulating his personal beliefs regarding the range of available human experience and their necessary link to the unconscious economy, but rather, I think, our unspoken cultural belief that our choices—regarding what we do and even what we think—are limited to, and by, what can be bought.

As I shot out of the woods at the bottom of the logging road, with my cheeks flushed from pushing against the cold winter air, and my legs pleasantly fatigued from our journey, I was again reminded that the unconscious economy's power to define my life was in large part dependent on my granting it this power.

In other words, the power was *mine.*

[CHAPTER ELEVEN]

In which I lay it out.

I HAVE now spent the better part of 2 years in the frequent company of Erik Gillard and the even more frequent company of my thoughts regarding money and wealth. In full candor, I sometimes worry that 2 years is not enough, that even 2 *decades* might not be sufficient to fully unravel all the threads of my expectations and associations relating to these matters. These are threads that have been spun and woven for the better part of my life; they are like a cocoon I have wrapped around me, and at times I still find myself struggling to emerge from its embrace.

I call our society's way of life the "unconscious economy" and the way of life I'm striving for the "conscious economy" because I fervently believe that the only sane way forward—indeed, the only *possible* way forward—is to become conscious of both our actions and our intent, and to understand the ramifications of each. We must awaken to the issues and then choose, with mindfulness and deliberate process, to move toward a personal economy that acknowledges and reveres true wealth. We must understand that this economy and wealth are not rooted in the language of money. They are *inclusive* of money, of course, but they return it to its rightful place by recognizing it for what it is: a tool; a means to an end, but never an end itself; a thing not inherently good or evil, but capable of being a conduit for either; and a poor substitute for the relationships and interconnectedness—in both the human and natural realm—it displaces.

People often ask how my life has changed as my views on money and wealth have changed, and this is a question that is at once very easy and very difficult to answer. The easy answer is that I feel liberated. The more I've let go of the notion that the accumulation of money should serve as a measure of my "success" or "failure" or even my "wealth," the closer I come to understanding the true definitions of these things. I don't know if the accumulation of money and an understanding of wealth as being something other than the accumulation of money are mutually exclusive; I suspect they are not. Surely there are people who are capable of holding each of these birds in a separate hand, never confusing one for the other. But that is not I, and, I suspect, it is not most of us. I have come to see how, in my life, the perception of money as a metric for my well-being tends to be a self-fulfilling prophecy: The more I believe the story it tells, the more I want to live this story. And the more I live it . . . well, you get the point.

But it's not really so simple, is it? Because of course I need money, as do you and as does pretty much everyone else on the planet. And in a sense, the freedom to reframe my relationship to money and wealth is the freedom of someone who is already privileged in these regards. I am not blind to this truth, or the irony inherent in it. We are all connected to the diseased system of contemporary monetary policy and the unconscious economy. We are all dependent on it for our very survival, and one of the highest tragedies of its sickness is that our dependence forces us to make decisions that only make us *more* dependent, as we continue to erode the underlying resource and relationship bases that form the core of a conscious economy.

To be clear: My interest is almost entirely on what can be done at a personal and community level to propagate a conscious economy. It is not that I don't believe there are systemic changes that can and should be made; indeed, there very much are, and for anyone interested in big picture thinking on these matters, I would again refer you to Charles Eisenstein's *Sacred Economics*. Eisenstein's thinking is at once logical, clear, and refreshing, and he's not afraid to put forth proposals that, were they to be adopted, would bring sweeping, transformational change to both our perception of wealth and our relationship to it.

That said, systemic change via our political organism has a frustrating tendency to take its own sweet time. This is the consequence of the cumbersome, layered nature of democracy, and the centuries of collectivism that have delivered us to this time and place. Generally speaking, it is only during times of chaos and outright crisis that our leaders move quickly, and even then they are hardly guaranteed to move in a healthy direction. As of this writing, the most recent example of this is the financial crisis of 2008, which of course only served to further the status quo and deepen our dependency on the unconscious economy by massively increasing the nation's debt load. Equally damaging is the continued assumption that we might "grow" our way out of the mess, as if doing more of the very thing that almost brought us to our knees will somehow deliver lasting rejuvenation.

It is funny how differently I interpret things now that I understand the conscious economy. No longer are reports of rising retail sales or increased manufacturing output or booming GDP numbers music to my ears. It is not so much that I *wish* for economic contraction and the inevitable suffering it visits upon us all. But the aforementioned metrics are merely offshoots of the unconscious economy, and their growth is no more reflective of our true health, wealth, and well-being than a three-beer buzz is to an alcoholic. In a very real sense, so-called improvements in these benchmarks are actually bad news, because the longer we rely on them to define our prosperity, the more dependent we become on the status quo. The real tragedy is not so much that the unconscious economy is poised to fail (although this is certainly true), but that it is utterly dependent on an ongoing crisis of exploitation, oppression, and outright robbery.

Still, the growth imperative remains the prevailing model, and because it is a model that disproportionately benefits those at the top of the income ladder,[42] it will not go gently into the dark night. Indeed, it is likely that we will only see increasing inequality as the unconscious economy continues to unwind and those who depend on its survival to maintain their archaic notion of wealth are compelled to hoard what remains. This situation will not last forever—our underlying resource base, not to mention the increasingly restless 99 percent, ensure that its days are numbered—but it might last longer than we can currently imagine. Already it has survived well beyond the time frame predicted by many.

All of this is not to say we should not work to bring the tenets of the conscious economy to the consciousness of the highest offices in the land. However, we would do well to remember who truly pulls the strings, and it is those who have the most to lose from this transition. Of course, they don't really have anything to lose, or at least, they have nothing of real value to lose, and only

---

[42] Naturally, these are the individuals and corporations that contribute the most to political campaigns.

true wealth to gain. But the *perception* that there would be loss, coupled with the considerable inertia of maintaining the status quo, leaves me skeptical that an institutionalized adoption of the conscious economy is likely to take place anytime before the cannibalistic destruction of its unconscious cousin.

Therefore, my inescapable conclusion is that it is up to us. If there is to be a near-term movement toward an economy that rejects the artificial security of accumulated tangible assets and embraces the true wealth of that which cannot be measured in dollars, it will begin at the individual level. But because we are as individuals connected to those around us, and because the conscious economy honors and strengthens these connections, to begin at the individual level is to begin at the communal level. That is the beauty of an economy that demands interconnectedness: It cannot happen in the vacuum of any individual's sphere. It is contagious.

All of this is well and good but admittedly a bit long on theory and short on specifics. So I return now to the question of how my life has changed as my views on money and wealth have evolved, and what follows is the difficult version of my answer. It is not difficult in the sense that it is hard to articulate; in truth, much of it quite readily lends itself to retelling. Instead, what makes it challenging is the understanding that what has been both applicable and possible for me, may not be so for others. It would be specious for me not to acknowledge the advantages and privileges I enjoy. Some are courtesy of my upbringing; some are the result of decisions made long ago. Ironically, at least a few have been directly enabled by the unconscious economy, which I have leveraged over the years to generate the income necessary to move more facets of my life into the realm of a conscious economy.

I make no claims to righteousness regarding my personal economic story. By necessity, I have my feet planted in both the conscious and unconscious economies and I know of no one—Erik

Gillard included—who can say differently. This duality is a necessary component of any transition, or of any smooth transition, at least. So I will not apologize for the contradictions that exist in relation to my economic sphere. They exist in part because I am responsible for the well-being of myself and my family, and in part because, frankly, there are elements of the unconscious economy that are simply too seductive to ignore. Have I given up driving, an act that, with its litany of externalized costs, is as embedded in the unconscious economy as any I can think of? Why, no, I haven't. Nor have I sworn off air travel, or technologies that exist only at the behest of the unconscious economy. I certainly did not scratch this manuscript into a cave wall with a sharp bit of stone. Of course, there are innumerable other ways in which I swim in the current of false abundance, so thoroughly has it infiltrated 21st-century American life.

So that's some of what *hasn't* changed in my life and, by extension, the lives of my family. Here's what has:

Given my newfound understanding of money creation, I am even more firmly resolved to avoid debt via the traditional channels (bank, credit card, finance companies, etc.). Whereas I once avoided these sources of debt strictly from a place of mild phobia and fear of sacrificing my autonomy in service of repayment, I now avoid them because I consider them to be damaging, not only to myself, but to the broader world. To dilute the money supply, while making excessive claims on the underlying resource base simply because I desire to "own" something that is beyond my means, no longer feels like a justifiable action. This is not to say there are not viable reasons to assume debt, reasons that fit within the context of a conscious economy. And it is a profoundly sad statement about the well-being of our nation that many people are forced to assume debt simply to acquire the most basic essentials of human survival. If ever there were evidence that money and commoditization have exceeded their proper boundaries, this is it.

I am not prepared to say that I would never again consider going into debt; only that if I were to procure a loan, it would be from a lender that does not leverage its reserves in order to create "money" out of thin air. Furthermore, excepting crisis situations, such as a health care or some other emergency, I cannot imagine assuming debt for anything that does not move me in the direction of economic consciousness. Which is to say, you will not soon see me behind the wheel of a new car, or sipping pina coladas on the deck of a cruise ship.

It occurs to me that of the many ways I am privileged, the luxury of choosing to avoid debt might be the most profound. The unconscious economy has largely stripped this privilege from our culture, and the very nature of interest-bearing debt all but ensures a treadmill of debt servitude that only the most diligent or fortunate can avoid. To be sure, my evasion of debt has taken a measure of both diligence *and* good fortune. And of course it didn't hurt that I married a woman willing to live without running water for years on end. Still, it is nonetheless true that a tremendous quantity of credit is extended for the purchase of nonessentials. Indeed, if we suddenly decided, en masse, to borrow *only* for life's true necessities of clothing, food, and shelter, our current economy would collapse. So while it is probable that not everyone can be so quick as myself to foreswear money-creating debt, it is equally probable that most can avoid exacerbating and extending the unconscious economy simply by swearing off debt for the purchase of nonessentials.

I have also come to understand how my accumulation of monetary wealth and other so-called financial assets is detrimental to the world beyond my door and, not inconsequently, to myself. But of all the conscious economy's tenets, I find that the nonaccumulation of money beyond my family's short-term needs is the thorniest to navigate. This is true for many reasons. First, we do not yet inhabit an entirely conscious economy, so the safety net of interdependence I spoke of earlier does not yet exist in full. Second, having been reared in contemporary America, I have been indoctrinated in the belief that such accumulation is worthy of my undivided attention and rigorous efforts and indeed is part and parcel of the so-called American Dream. Finally, I find that I cannot completely sever my emotional trigger in regard to money. It's as if each opportunity to cash in transforms me into one of Pavlov's hapless subjects. I ring the bell and sit up smartly, waiting obediently for my reward.

There are innumerable justifications for monetary accumulation beyond my immediate needs, but the one that triggers the most emotional vulnerability is the simple fact that I have children; is it not my duty to protect them from the unpredictability of this cold, cruel world? Is it not my duty to provide for them, to maintain a reserve to be tapped in the event of some unforeseen emergency? I believe it is, but an obvious question arises: *How much is enough?* Five thousand dollars? Ten thousand? One hundred thousand? A half million? There is no clear answer, and therefore, no correct answer, and I know from personal experience that no amount—or, at least, no amount that I've been able to amass—ever feels like enough. I can recount specific instances when we've had $1,000 in savings and I've thought, "If only we had $2,000, I'd feel secure." And then $2,000 comes and I can't help thinking that $3,000 would make me feel just a wee more comfortable. You can see where I'm going with this, can't you? I suppose there might be an upper end to this line of thought—I mean, is it possible that, say, Warren Buffet frets over his nest egg? Frankly, I think it *is* possible, but even if it's not, I hardly need point out that Warren Buffet is as extreme an example as exists, and that there's a hell of a lot of daylight between my family's modest savings (and, I'm betting, yours) and Buffet's fantastically out-sized holdings.

At this point, I hardly need to point out that in a fully conscious economy, the very unpredictability I would seek to shield my children from would be largely mitigated. This would be true on a personal and regional level, where I could rely on the interconnectedness of my community to provide the support the unconscious economy forces me to purchase. But to an extent, it would also be true on a national and even global scale, where the adoption of a conscious economy would significantly reduce the risk of such unpredictability in the first place. In a conscious economy, the hazards of the contemporary global condition, in which there is significant tension caused by the hoarding of resources and competition for economic, political, and military dominance, has given way to peaceful interdependence. Indeed, one can see clear parallels between how the unconscious economy functions on both global and individual levels; the issues and damages are very much the same. Only the scale and scope are different.

Still, none of this resolves the fact that, much as we might wish otherwise, the unconscious economy currently dominates and, much as we might wish otherwise, we cannot simply choose to live beyond the reach of its laws, both written and unwritten. And so the question pertaining to the accumulation of monetary wealth lingers: how to resolve the conflict between what I wish for and the reality I must navigate? The answer to this question deserves some detail, because of course this is a question that is central to every one of the conscious economy's tenets: Namely, how does one move in a direction that one knows to be correct and healthy for humanity at large when doing so creates a degree of vulnerability that must be borne by the individual?

In truth, there *is* a short answer to this question, at least for my family and myself. It is perhaps a little snarky, but no less the honest for being so: How does one *not* move in a direction that one knows to be correct and healthy for humanity at large? For us, at least, it has become untenable to not do everything within our power to move toward a conscious economy, even in the context of widespread and entrenched arrangements that all but ensure such movement will at times feel treacherous.

That's the short answer. Here is the long one.

Regarding money, we have generally chosen to not accumulate more than we might reasonably need as a buffer against unanticipated expenses. Given that we carry no debt, and are able to provide many of the basic essentials for ourselves on our farm, this figure is probably lower than it will be for someone in a more typical financial arrangement. On the other hand, considering the inconsistent paychecks inherent to my line of work, we do feel compelled to maintain enough savings to see us through a lean month or two.

The conversation regarding monetary accumulation would not be complete without distinguishing between accumulation solely for the purpose of so-called "security" in an unknowable future and saving toward a well-defined goal that moves one in a positive direction. This is not to say that saving for retirement is not valid; indeed, if it is your life dream to ensure that your twilight years are met with monetary abundance, and you are content making the necessary sacrifices now to meet your expectations for the future, well then, go for it. I am not here to tell you that your dream is any less valid than mine, or than anyone else's.

But no matter what you are saving for, this is what I suggest: Do not save money out of fear. Instead, save money only when saving money is going to help you realize a dream or take a step toward that dream. Accumulate money only once you have asked yourself if what you are accumulating it for is worth more to you than the portion of your life being exchanged for those symbolic units of value. I have not forgotten Erik's unlikely math lesson, learned during his internal debate over whether or not to purchase his bicycle. *"And then I realized that the price equaled six workdays; six days in the woods with kids. Would I trade six days in the woods for this beautiful bike? I realized I would, and it affirmed to me that I am living a right lifestyle."* Simply reminding myself that each purchasing decision is in reality a decision to exchange a fraction of my life for a particular item has been enough to profoundly alter my consumptive patterns.

We have chosen to not put a hard ceiling on how much money we will earn, although it is interesting to note that in the second year of my writing this book, I earned $37,428, very near the $35,145 I pulled down in year one. We have become exceptionally comfortable on this income, and the current thinking is that we could live handsomely on much less. Indeed, we are moving in that direction, with the intention that whatever income we do not need to meet daily expenses will be applied toward our goal of establishing a conscious economy by allowing it to flow through us.

This warrants further explanation, if for no other reason than it might sound a bit specious to leverage the unconscious economy's monetary wealth for the purpose of building a conscious economy. But I stand firm in my conviction that money, both in concept and physical construct, is not the problem: The problem is intent; the problem is how we use money, and what we expect of it.

Therefore, our intent for monetary wealth in excess of our daily needs is to find ways in which it might build upon the portion of our economy that is tilting toward consciousness. This could mean interest-free loans to friends who need capital; it could mean investments that allow us to produce more nourishment on our small farm, to be made available to our community. Lately, we have been planting fruit and nut trees, and if there's a more humbling acknowledgment of my own mortality than planting a bareroot nut tree that is not likely to produce in my lifetime, I'm not sure what it is. And we have been investing heavily in our farm's depleted soils, returning them to health with minerals and organic fertilizers.

I know that some will find it downright irresponsible that we are not investing this money in retirement accounts and college savings plans, and I must confess, there are times when we question the wisdom of not doing so. We live in a society that refuses to acknowledge the holistic wealth that is embodied in our trees and soil. Indeed, these are "investments," for both will surely return what we have put into them, and more so. But of course they are not recognized as such, and their returns will not be accepted as currency for a great many of the things we need in a commodity marketplace. If one of my children falls ill and requires medical care, I can't just show up at the hospital with a bushel of apples to exchange for treatment.

This is the thorniest factor in moving my family's life in the direction of a conscious economy; namely, I cannot control the reality that most of the economy still operates in an unconscious sphere and the fact that, much as I might wish otherwise, I remain dependent on commodified goods and services and the monetized relationships they give rise to. This vulnerability is particularly acute in the realm of health care, which has become so fantastically expensive that many people spend large portions of their lives working jobs they can't stand just so they can maintain the health benefits provided by those jobs.

Still, it must be acknowledged that many of our current health woes are a direct result of the unconscious economy. For instance, the incidence of type 2 diabetes has *tripled* in some age groups over just the past 4 decades, and the Centers for Disease Control and Prevention predicts that as many as one-third of adults could have diabetes by 2050. Not surprisingly, diabetes has become an enormously profitable disease for the pharmaceutical industry, with Americans spending $100 billion on treatment annually.

The question, of course, is why diabetes (to name just one of a plethora of diseases that are currently skyrocketing) is becoming so prevalent. The answer in large part is the rapid evolution of our commodity food system toward cheap and generously subsidized crops like corn and soy. Is it any coincidence that the tripling in type 2 diabetes rates occurred over the same period during which consumption of high fructose corn syrup rose from approximately 4 pounds to 40 pounds annually per capita?

While it is true that I cannot protect my family from every single health crisis, it is true that by making informed decisions about how we eat and otherwise care for ourselves, we can absolve ourselves of much of the risk associated with the contemporary American lifestyle. We place tremendous importance on the quality of the food we consume, and on ensuring that our lives remain as stress free and full of beauty as possible. These factors, as much as anything else, provide our "health insurance."

Of course, some portion of my life must by necessity remain tethered to the unconscious economy. This is indisputable, and there is no calculation that can show me what portion of my life this should be. Instead, I rely on intuition and a simple question that never fails to provide guidance when I find myself at a crossroads: *What am I agreeing to?* And, when faced with a choice—to invest in a mutual fund or in nut trees, to buy a new car or keep patching the rust holes on the old one, to borrow a tool from a neighbor or buy one for myself—what does my decision tell me about what I am agreeing to? Am I agreeing to the world I want to inhabit, or am I capitulating to the prevailing story of the commodity economy? Of course, there are times it must be the latter, but as I have found both in my life and in observing Erik's, the more I agree to inhabit a conscious economy, the more opportunities I have to reject the commodified status quo.

Still, despite the emotional and intellectual gyrations associated with attempting to define the monetary aspect of my life, this is only part of the story. To be sure, it is a part that deserves serious consideration, if for no other reason than my responsibility to provide for my family. But to allow financial considerations to dominate is both tragic and ironic because the greatest benefits bestowed by the conscious economy have little to do with money.

Indeed, what I have observed in both Erik's life and my own is the extent to which money's relevance wanes as we begin to understand what a poor representation of wealth it truly is. Or maybe it only wanes in relation to the other components of holistic wealth, as they come to command increasingly large portions of our total affluence pie. In other words, it's hard to care so much about money when you care so much about other people, or when you truly understand that how you spend your hours is how you spend your life. It's hard to care so much about money when you inhabit each moment so thoroughly that you have little emotional or intellectual space left over to fret about tomorrow, next week, next year, and so on. It's hard to care so much about money when you recognize that caring so much about money is driving a wedge between yourself and the things that are *really* deserving of your care: personal relationships, the natural world, your freedom and spirit. It's hard to care so much about money when you have found alternative ways to secure at least some of the basic essentials of human survival. When, to put it simply, you aren't *scared*.

It is a largely unacknowledged truth that the contemporary American life is lived under a guillotine of fear. We fear disease, poverty, terrorism, loneliness, and death. We spend a lifetime seeking security because we are told the world is an insecure and dangerous place; that peril lurks around each corner. We spend so much of our time believing these fears and trying to abate them that we don't even stop to consider whether our anxieties might be misplaced. We don't even wonder if perhaps the things we fear are, at least in part, the tragic outgrowth of our misguided attempts to create an artifice of security. We have disease because we have allowed our food to be commoditized and thus subject to the profit-borne whims of corporatism; we have poverty because we have believed the lie that money buys security and because we have created a system that unjustly allows money to beget money; we have terrorism largely because we have meddled and assumed the righteous stance of American exceptionalism; we have loneliness because we no longer need one another; we have death because it is inevitable, and we know this, yet because we have come to see ourselves as separate from nature and its laws, we believe that death is something to be vanquished. It has become a foe. And until we have conquered our foes, we fear them.

It is fascinating to me to consider the evolution of this story. I'd originally wanted merely to better understand money, and I wound up better understanding the ways in which I relate to the world around me. It is no exaggeration to say I wound up better understanding *myself*. Because once you peel back the illusory nature of the wealth and security our contemporary monetary policy and economic expectations provide, you are forced to confront the truth: We are all connected, and we are all meant to be connected, both to one another, and to the natural world that underpins our existence. To live amidst the false abundance of a system that exchanges our true wealth for accumulated tokens of prosperity might, for a time, provide a sense of comfort and satisfaction. Of well-being. But that sense of well-being is no more durable than the inherent worth of the bills and digits used to represent it.

It is not that we need to abandon money; it is that we need to return it to its rightful role as merely one of numerous means of exchange, and never a means to an end. We need to understand that money by itself is nothing. It is a creation, a story, a rabbit pulled out of a hat, and yet it wields the power to cause irreparable damage. This may sound counterintuitive, but it is precisely money's nothingness that lends it such power, for it is this quality that allows it to be infinite in a finite world. We must use money in full consciousness of this power. We must accept that we have granted it this capacity, and that anything we have granted can just as easily be rescinded.

This includes the power it wields over us, with its unique capacity to hold us captive, in mind and body. The most remarkable change in my life since I began to break from money's spell is a profound sense of freedom and choice as I sink deeper into the understanding that my life need not be defined by money and the pursuit of wealth. Much like Erik, I have come to realize the extent to which it is my privilege to experience this freedom and choice, and try not to take it for granted. I am grateful for it, and I notice how the more grateful I feel, the more money's spell wanes. I notice how the less I fret over money, the less I need to fret over money because I find myself more connected to the things that truly matter, for which money will always be a poor substitute. In other words, I do not even want what I once wanted. I do not want what the marketplace tells me I should want.

This is going to sound painfully obvious, but here it is, anyway: This is your *life*. This is your *one* life, and the incredibly, amazingly beautiful thing about it is that *you* get to choose how to spend it. It is true that those of us with children carry the added responsibility of knowing our choices regarding how we spend our lives are by default choices regarding how they spend their lives. But in all sincerity, I ask this simple question: Are your children better off having you work the long days necessary to provide them the "opportunities" we've been conditioned to provide, or are they better off simply having you? Because you will not get another chance to be with your children, or for that matter, any of your loved ones.

What is it that compels us to consistently choose the path we've been taught to choose? Fear, as we've discussed. And, I've come to believe, a misplaced assumption that we inhabit a world beset by scarcity and that we must gird ourselves against this scarcity. For most of my life, I believed in scarcity, but now I see that scarcity, like money itself, is merely a story we are told, and I view the world as being amazingly, almost impossibly abundant. In many ways this is the most affecting aspect of my shifting consciousness, and I view it as a tremendous gift: to see plenty where I once saw paucity and to understand how truly generous and gracious nature is. My view of people has been similarly altered, although of course many cling to the worldview proffered by the unconscious economy, and they often feel as if they cannot afford to be as generous and gracious as their spirits whisper is possible.

But how can I blame them? After all, they live the tragic irony that the myth of scarcity drives the reality of scarcity for those who cannot afford to participate in an economy that has monetized and commoditized almost every basic human need. There is plenty for all, but fed by fear, marketing, and flawed assumptions, those who are able to do so consume and accumulate vastly more than they need, ensuring that we inhabit a world of massive inequality, where scarcity is manufactured by arrangements that are hardly questioned. Indeed, we have been indoctrinated to the myth of scarcity in no small part because a world of abundance is a world in which monopolistic corporate entities make no sense. It is a world in which hierarchal socioeconomic stratification makes no sense. It is a world in which fear makes no sense.

There is no question that abandoning the quest for accumulated monetary wealth carries with it a degree of risk. But life is riddled with risk, which the accumulation of monetary wealth seems to mitigate only because so many experiences and aspects of human survival have become commodified: Birth. Death. Food. Water. Even the very air we breathe has fallen victim to the unconscious economy, as it is increasingly sullied by fallout from industry.[43] The monetary arrangements we have established enable us to exchange our money for our freedom, at least to a certain extent, but it is a specific type of freedom. It is, as Lewis Hyde describes, "a catalog of possible lives," with each possibility affixed with a price tag. In other words, it is a *conditional* freedom and freedom, like love, cannot be both conditional and pure.

I have learned—I am still learning—to accept the risk that comes of embracing an alternate freedom because increasingly it feels to me as if the freedom offered by the unconscious economy is both tenuous and insincere. Increasingly, it feels to me as if maintaining the illusion of abundance contained within Hyde's catalog of possible lives is keeping me from realizing the true wealth of interconnectedness, and that the greater risk lies in never knowing the richness and simple joy of this interconnectedness.

---

[43] In the United States, asthma is the fastest-growing chronic disease, claiming 4,000 lives annually.

It is true that neither Erik nor myself have managed to decouple ourselves from the illusory abundance of the unconscious economy, and I do not expect that we ever will. But I have also learned that this is not an all-or-nothing endeavor, and that the catalog of possible lives can be extended to include those experiences and relationships that fall outside the unconscious economy. It is as if there are two parallel economies, one conscious and one not, and it feels as if the most important thing I can do for myself and others is try my damndest to build a bridge between the two.

I recall something Erik once told me, one of the few things I've heard him say that I actually disagree with. It was during the afternoon we plastered the interior walls of his cabin, after the night he'd spent roaming by foot, fretting that simply by living in accordance with his values, he wasn't affecting change. Or enough change, at least. "My lifestyle is just a lifestyle choice. It's not a strategy that's going to affect things on a systemic level."

If Erik lived in a vacuum, that might be so. But of course he does not live in a vacuum; he inhabits a community that is itself part of a larger community that is part of something even larger. And so on. Erik might dismiss the choices he has made and continues to make as "lifestyle choices," but to me, they are much more than that. I think of them as pebbles dropped into a pool, and I see how they ripple through the lives of those around him, informing and even enabling their choices. I think of how my life has been affected by those ripples: I have become more generous, less fearful, and increasingly content. Where I once saw scarcity, I now see plenty. I feel more connected to those around me and to the natural order, both as embodied by the physical structure of the land on which I live, and the too-often unacknowledged truth that my humanness does not grant me permission to stand apart from it. I am separate from nothing.

We are repeatedly told that the path to prosperity and contentment is the one paved by the commodity economy, the one that separates and compartmentalizes us. We have been told this so often, for so long, that sometimes we forget to take our eyes off the path, to look up and around. To look forward. To look *inward*. To feel that separation and acknowledge the toll it takes.

This is what I humbly suggest. For at least a moment, forget everything you know and have been told about money and wealth and abundance and how they should inform your life. Forget, even, everything you have read in the preceding pages, and simply grant yourself the gift of allowing your mind and heart to expand beyond the range of what you've been told is desirable. Or even possible. And at the same time you are forgetting all of this, remember this simple truth: The manner in which you pass your time is the manner in which you pass your life.

How, then, do you want to *live*?

And so I came to spend a small fraction of my life hunched over a pair of overturned plastic buckets just outside the front door of Erik's cabin, running a handsaw through a slab of salvaged two-by-ten, and wishing he'd held on to our chop saw for a while longer. It was early May and the day was serene, warm, and breezeless, the clouds puffs of cotton in the sky. The exact date was May 9, which I know because I'd written it in my notebook but also because it was Erik's 28th birthday. As such, there was to be a gathering at the cabin that evening, and it was decided that a set of front steps was needed to replace the precarious slab-of-plywood-perched-atop-a-couple-of-stumps-and-a-moldy-haybale arrangement that had served him for the past year or so.

Erik was still living at Heidi's, although he no longer referred to it as such, instead calling it "our place." At some point over the past couple of months, he had cut his hair short and trimmed his beard to a fashionably neat goatee. It was amazing what the grooming did for him; it wasn't as if he'd been a slob before, but now he looked downright dapper. In another set of clothes, he could have fit in at any brokerage or law firm. But of course he wore his usual assemblage of thrift-store attire, with his usual baseball cap perched atop his newly shorn head. The cap sat high and slightly off-center, and, worn thusly, reminded me of the prow of a great seafaring vessel.

I was pleased to see that Erik hadn't given up on the cabin. Over the preceding months, he'd finished plastering the walls and even cleaned most of the excess plaster from the beams and floor. And he'd applied whitewash over the plaster, which had brightened the place significantly. There was still plenty to be done, of course: finish floors, trim, some sort of paneling for upstairs walls and ceiling. Cardboard had been considered ("It'd be fun to draw on," he told me)—and then dismissed. Whatever he decided on, I was pretty sure it wouldn't be typical. Or expensive.

What would he do with the cabin, now that it needn't provide his day-in, day-out shelter? He didn't know, exactly, but thought it might make a nice art studio, or perhaps a place to stay for visiting friends. I thought of the bucket toilet, but even as I did I realized that Erik did not consort with the sort of people who would think twice about bathrooming out-of-doors, or reading by candlelight. In any event, Erik's enthusiasm for the structure seemed undiminished, and his pride in his progress was evident. "It's really coming along," he'd told me a few days before, his voice bright with the simple satisfaction of it all.

The decision to construct steps had been arrived at only after some consideration and a brief debate regarding priorities. "What do you think?" asked Erik when I arrived. "Should we make a platform for the bathtub"—he motioned to an old cast-iron tub straddling the line between forest and cabin clearing—"so we can light a fire under it and do some hot-tubbing, or should we build some steps?" Even as he mentioned the steps, his gaze lingered on the tub, and I knew in which direction he was leaning. Clearly, I would need to be the voice of reason: He'd invited 30 people, some of whom had never been to his cabin. Furthermore, much of the party would take place under the cloak of night, and of course, he had no lights. The plywood-stump-hay contraption was profoundly sketchy even in the full reveal of day. A wood-fired bathtub-turned-hot-tub would be a pleasing novelty and was, for lack of a better term, very "Erik." But steps? Given the circumstances, they were essential.

To my great surprise, Erik acquiesced to my pragmatism and in short order we had begun construction on a set of rudimentary stairs, utilizing haphazard pieces of lumber he'd stashed along the cabin's northern wall. We tugged them out one by one, as the whole pile teetered precariously. Once cut to the proper length with the handsaw, we fastened the boards together with the least-bent of the used screws he'd been collecting in an old yogurt container. Despite the well-worn nature of his materials, and the 19th-century cutting technology, it took us less than an hour to complete the project, making ingress and egress to his cabin a relatively simple (and safe) affair.

We stood back to admire our handiwork. It was a fine piece of work. Well, maybe not exactly "fine," because in truth the middle step seemed to tilt a bit from left to right. Or maybe it was the bottom step that tilted from right to left; whatever the case, the relationship between the two seemed a bit out of whack. And to be honest, I harbored some minor concerns regarding the holding power of the repurposed screws we'd used. Might they have been compromised by their previous task? There was no way to know for certain, but it seemed possible. Still, vigorous stomping on my part did not expose any acute structural defects, and the project was deemed a success.

In fact, things had gone so smashingly that we found ourselves with a spare hour or two before Erik was due back at Heidi's, where he was to be led on a long and convoluted treasure hunt that would culminate with his birthday gift.[44] It was not quite enough time to tackle the wood-fired bathtub contraption, but it was plenty enough to motor up a long, winding hill to the north, where almost a year before we'd found hatfuls and shirtfuls of morel mushrooms with Erik's friend Breakfast.

Erik offered to drive, so we hopped into the little Honda he and Heidi had recently procured. It was a replacement for her truck, which still sat in the driveway, having been diagnosed with a blown head gasket. The car was exactly what I would have expected Erik to own, if he were to own any car at all; it was small and thrifty, and bore a coat of blue paint, weathered by nearly 15 years of exposure to the elements. The interior was in great disarray, with scraps of paper and other detritus scattered about. I counted $1.68 in spare change sprinkled across the floor like confetti, and that was without looking under the seats.

Unlike my previous experience with him piloting an automobile, Erik drove ploddingly and he seemed unaware of the fact that his windshield wipers were swishing uselessly across a dry windshield. We passed a chicken, meandering aimlessly along the road's shoulder. We passed a young child on a bicycle, meandering aimlessly along the road's shoulder. The leaves on the trees were just emerging from their buds, and the whole world seemed ready to explode to green. We passed Heidi's house, where the lawn had been almost entirely converted to garden space. A gaggle of ducks quacked and waddled about inside a square of fence. Two others were splashing in a shallow pool that had been dug by hand. The intent was to grow rice in the pool. Growing rice in Vermont . . . I tried to muster surprise, but could not.

As he drove, Erik talked about the bicycle tour he was helping organize. It was called the "Solar Rollers," and his participation

---

[44] This would turn out to be a used clarinet, which I should not have been surprised to learn Erik played with surprising skill.

in both its orchestration and actual undertaking were part of his efforts to help shut down Vermont Yankee, the state's only nuclear power plant. For the bike tour, he'd created a whimsical promotional poster, featuring a quartet of wild animals—a fox, a raccoon, a turtle, and a bird that might have been a blue jay—piloting bicycles against a backdrop of green hills. The making of the poster had been somewhat stressful for him, primarily because it had necessitated a fair amount of computer time. "When I'm at a computer, I feel like my life's wasting away. I mean literally, viscerally." He made a fluttering motion with one hand, like a bird taking flight.

Still, his efforts in protesting the nuclear power plant seemed to have abated, at least temporarily, the gnawing sensation he'd experienced the previous November. "I think I have to go beyond the lifestyle," he'd told me then, after a sleepless night spent wandering the streets of his small town, wondering if his limited participation in the commodity economy was enough to affect positive change in the broader world. True, he hadn't managed to shutter the nuclear facility, and he acknowledged the work was frustratingly lacking in tangible progress, but the mere fact that he was doing *something* was enough to stem the tide of self-recrimination. "I couldn't live with myself if I wasn't trying," he told me. He repeated it: "I couldn't live with myself."

Meanwhile, his avoidance of money had, if anything, picked up steam. Just a few weeks before, in April, he'd paid a visit to the local health clinic to have his teeth cleaned. The clinic structured its fees on a sliding scale in relation to income, so Erik had completed an income statement at the outset of his visit, and handed it to the receptionist. "This can't be right," the receptionist said, when she examined Erik's paperwork. "It says here you've only made $300 so far this year."

It was, of course, correct; in the 3 months that had passed since the start of the New Year, Erik had made a mere $300, occasionally working at the wilderness day camp he'd long been a part of, and also at a friend's fledgling nursery. "But I have to find some more work soon," he admitted. "I don't have much money left." I cast my gaze around the interior of the Honda, and wondered how long it would take him to realize he had at least $1.68 in spare change sloshing around the car. Heck, it was probably enough to last him a week.

A dozen or so minutes after we left the cabin, we pulled onto the same steep gravel road we'd visited the year before, and beelined for the same reliably prolific copse of dead elm trees where, 12 months earlier, I'd harvested my first-ever morels. With the benefit of a full season of mushrooming under my belt, I felt none of the uncertainty I'd felt the previous year: I knew what to look for and if they were there, I'd find them, damn it.

Except, they weren't there. We scoured the ground beneath the elms, finding nothing but a layer of leaves shed the autumn before and gone brown and brittle. The leaves crackled and crunched under our feet, as if we were walking on a thin sheet of glass. We moved on to another spot, a bit deeper into the forest. We climbed up a sharp rise, then across. I could feel the pulse of my blood moving through my body. It felt good. I could smell the arrival of spring, the sweet muskiness of the decomposing organic matter that carpeted the ground and, floating on top of it, something lighter, almost floral. The expanding buds of the trees, perhaps, opening to see sun for the first time.

Still, we did not find mushrooms. "Maybe it's too early," said Erik. He scratched an armpit. "The weather is so screwed up this year." We poked around for another minute, to no avail. And then, just as I was preparing to climb farther up the hill, to the abandoned apple orchard that lined the path Erik once walked daily on his way to and from the cabin in the woods, he spoke again. "I've probably got to be getting back. Do you know what time it is?"

Funny, I had no idea.

THE CONSCIOUS ECONOMY MANIFESTO

- **IN A CONSCIOUS ECONOMY,** there is widespread recognition that one's time is, in truth, one's life. This cultivates a degree of self-respect and self-reverence that is largely absent from the unconscious economy, where so much of our life is spent at jobs we despise, or in mindless passivity.[45]
- **IN A CONSCIOUS ECONOMY,** no one believes the idiom that time is money. This is not to say that no one works for an hourly wage, only that one does so with the presence of mind that it is not merely one's time being sold, but one's life. As such, purchases are made with utmost consideration for not merely their commodity value, but their worth in relation to that which is their true cost: a percentage of one's finite waking hours upon this earth.
- **IN A CONSCIOUS ECONOMY,** material objects are valued for both their utilitarian capacity and the personal connections they represent. The resources they embody are acknowledged, and from that acknowledgment comes respect and gratitude for the gift of these resources. Furthermore, there is widespread awareness that the consumption of nonrenewable resources means that others cannot benefit from their use. As such, we enter into a new era of consummate materialism, rooted in quality, rather than quantity. Maintenance and care of material objects are part and parcel of this materialism.

---

[45] Needless to say, the role of television and media in the conscious economy is greatly reduced.

- **IN A CONSCIOUS ECONOMY,** it is understood that the health of the economy cannot be accurately assessed by numerical metrics such as gross domestic product because such metrics are a product of commoditization. Instead, the "economy" component incorporates numerous elements beyond the realms of money and finance. These include, but are not limited to, self-assessed measures of happiness and contentment, job satisfaction, physical health, soil health, access to nourishing foods, and the overall well-being of the environment.
- **IN A CONSCIOUS ECONOMY,** it is clear to all that the money-as-debt model is inherently unstable and unsustainable. The capacity to loan money into existence, to be repaid with interest, creates a dynamic of ever-increasing claims on our underlying resource base: our "true wealth," if you will. There is widespread awareness that this type of debt fails us on every level, from the moral to the structural vulnerability it generates in the systemic arrangements we depend upon for our day-to-day survival.
- **IN A CONSCIOUS ECONOMY,** money is only one of many tools that allow us to conduct exchange and store value. Furthermore, it is understood that money's value is merely representative, and that it always represents the underlying resources, be they of nature or humankind, to which it ultimately lays claim. As such, money is not seen as a means to an end, but rather a medium through which to obtain these resources.
- **IN A CONSCIOUS ECONOMY,** the true costs associated with all forms of production are diligently sought. These costs include but are not limited to: the energy embedded in products and services, environmental degradation, and the humanitarian toll often associated with the extraction

of natural resources and industrial manufacture. As an honest accounting of these factors is sought, these processes will become increasingly regionalized, so that accountability cannot be diluted by distance.

- **IN A CONSCIOUS ECONOMY,** there is a clear distinction between "value" and "worth." The former is used for items and services that exist in the commodity marketplace and must by necessity be priced against a dislike metric; the latter applies to items and elements that cannot be readily assigned a market value. It is broadly understood that "value" is subject to external forces beyond individual control, while "worth" is more autonomous and, therefore, more secure.
- **IN A CONSCIOUS ECONOMY,** personal interconnectedness and interdependence are embraced, and the prevailing ethos of self-reliance is shunned. To rely on others is not considered shameful, nor does doing so result in accrued debt. Because of the increased social engagement demanded by interdependence, there is less anonymity and more personal accountability, and as a result social pressure ensures that few exploit this "system" of generosity. It is from this emerging culture of interdependence that a portion of our needs are met outside the scope of the dominant money system, and our concept of "social security" evolves to include the strength and resilience of our relationships with those around us.
- **IN A CONSCIOUS ECONOMY,** we are wealthy in what matters, and poor (or at least, poorer) in what doesn't. It is generally understood that what matters is nature, relationships, community, freedom, spiritual fulfillment, and overall contentment. Likewise, it is generally understood that what doesn't matter is the accumulation of money

and the collection of anonymous, homogenized goods that, despite all promises to the contrary, only demean and dilute our relationships to that which does matter. This will require many of us to accept a lower "standard of living," as defined by the unconscious economy. However, while divesting ourselves of the accumulated abundance in Things That Do Not Matter is likely to foment a degree of emotional unease, this unease will ultimately be offset by the embrace of Things That Do Matter and the simple pleasure of inviting them into our lives.

- **IN A CONSCIOUS ECONOMY,** there is no "too big to fail" among the institutions that provide the goods and services of contemporary American life. This is because there is no dependence on vulnerable institutions that are allowed to attain such power and influence in the first place.
- **IN A CONSCIOUS ECONOMY,** we can afford to pursue our passions and discover our true gift to the world. And because we are no longer consumed with the accumulation of monetary wealth, we are freer in emotion and intellect. Not only does our time (life) become our own again, so to do our thoughts and feelings.
- **IN A CONSCIOUS ECONOMY,** there is no separation between "us" and "nature" or between some of "us" and others of "us" or between the physical and spiritual representations of "us." As such, there is broad acceptance of the truism that our well-being is dependent on the well-being of elements that are commonly viewed as distinct and separate from the physical embodiment of the human form and all its thoughts and actions.
- **IN A CONSCIOUS ECONOMY,** it is understood that the contemporary view of life and death as divergent and autonomous states is a contrivance of human emotion, and

> it is acknowledged that, in accordance with the law of nature, each is dependent on the other. This is important because often it is our fear of personal decline and inevitable death that creates a sense of panicked vulnerability. In an unconscious economy, this vulnerability is often treated with consumption, accumulation, and other compulsions. As we move toward an economy in which we see life and death as being not just two sides of the same coin, but events along the continuum of human existence, we become less vulnerable and less fearful, and therefore more able to fully appreciate whatever time we are allotted.

When taken as a whole, the Conscious Economy Manifesto might seem overwhelming or perhaps idealistic. But its true power lies in the fact that it is more process than prescription, and that adopting even a single tenet can have a profound impact in how one views the world and the choices one makes to align one's life with that view.

To those who doubt that individual choice can affect the sort of change that so desperately needs to happen on a national and even global scale, I ask that you consider how your actions might influence others. I ask that you remember how Erik, with the quiet activism of his personal decisions, has managed to so profoundly impact my life and the lives of many around him. Already in his young life, he has dropped many pebbles, and those pebbles have generated many waves.

Maybe it's time for you to drop some pebbles of your own.